Why Pocket Posters?

Daydream Education, the UK's leading provider of educational posters, has developed a versatile range of colourful and engaging revision guides that break down barriers to learning and encourage independent learning.

Small in size, huge in content!

Our Religious Studies Pocket Posters cover core religious beliefs, teachings and practices to help pupils develop a deeper understanding of religion. The pocket-sized revision guides simplify curriculum topics and encourage students to engage effectively with different religions and religious issues.

POCKET POSTERS

66 I love Daydream Education's Pocket Posters as they provide clear and concise information. It means the students can find exactly what they need quickly and get to applying it. 99

Barry Dunn
Religious Studies Teacher

Daydream Education | Unit 1 | Central Park | Western Avenue | Bridgend | CF31 3RH
Tel: 0844 800 1660 | Fax: 0844 800 1664 | www.daydreameducation.co.uk
Chris Malcolm Ltd. t/a Daydream Education. Registered in England and Wales. Company No: 04216204

GCSE Religious Studies

Contents

✝ I am a Christian

Christians are the followers of Jesus Christ. Christians believe the Bible is the Word of God.

God

I believe in God who is represented as a Trinity: God the Father, God the Son and God the Holy Spirit. I believe that God came down to Earth in human form as Jesus, to die on the cross and absolve me of sin.

Worship

As a Christian, I pray at church and at home. Prayer is a way of worshipping, giving thanks to and communicating with God.

Christian Leaders

Priests, vicars or ministers lead worship in Christian ceremonies. They can have a huge impact on the community, bringing it together.

Holy Book

The Bible (New Testament) is important to me as it shows Christians how we should live our lives. It contains the Gospels of Matthew, Mark, Luke and John which tell the story of Jesus's life.

Easter

At Easter, I celebrate the resurrection of Jesus Christ from the dead. Easter is the most important Christian festival.

Pilgrimage

Pilgrimage is a journey to a sacred place, such as Lourdes or Iona, to show religious devotion. The Virgin Mary appeared to Marie-Bernarde "Bernadette" Soubirous at Lourdes. Iona has always been seen as a holy place where saints have lived.

Christmas

Christmas is a Christian festival that recognises the birth of Jesus. Christmas is acknowledged annually on December 25th and celebrated by billions of people around the world.

Sacraments

We celebrate the Sacraments (holy rituals) of Baptism and Holy Communion. These signify joining God's family as a Christian and accepting Jesus into our life.

Catholics

Catholics are members of the Roman Catholic Church. They follow the teachings of the Bible and sacred Roman Catholic traditions. The Pope is the leader of the Catholic Church, and Catholics believe that the Pope is the successor of the Apostle Peter (the first head of the Church, who was appointed by Jesus). Therefore, they believe in the authority and teachings of the Pope.

Protestants

Protestantism originated in 1517 with the Protestant Reformation; a revolt against the control of the Roman Catholic Church. Protestants believe that the Bible alone is the source of God's special revelation to mankind and is the standard by which all Christian behaviour must be measured. They reject all other authorities, such as Church traditions and the Pope.

Eastern Orthodox Christians

The Eastern Orthodox Church split from the Catholic Church in 1054 due to conflicting views on the structure and governance of the Church. The split was known as the East–West Schism.

Creation

Christians believe that God created all things. The story of creation is found in the book of Genesis, Chapter 1, and describes how God created the world and everything in it.

Christians believe that God created the world in six days and rested on the seventh.

Day 1

DARKNESS | LIGHT

God created light and dark.

Day 2

God created the sky.

Day 3

God created earth, oceans and plants.

Day 4

God created the sun, moon and stars.

Day 5

God created all sea life and birds.

Day 6

God created people and animals.

Day 7

God rested.

'In the beginning was the Word, and the Word was with God, and the Word was God. He was with God in the beginning. Through him all things were made; without him nothing was made that has been made.' **(John 1:1-3, NIV)**

In the passage above, 'the Word' is believed to be a reference to the Son of God, Jesus Christ, and introduces the idea of God as the Trinity. The Holy Spirit aspect of God is also referred to:

"In the beginning God created the heavens and the earth. Now the earth was formless and empty, darkness was over the surface of the deep, and the Spirit of God was hovering over the waters. And God said, 'Let there be light,' and there was light." **(Genesis 1:1-3, NIV)**

A further example of God as the Trinity is highlighted when God refers to Himself in the plural:

"Then God said, 'Let us make mankind in our image, in our likeness, so that they may rule over the fish in the sea and the birds in the sky...'" **(Genesis 1:26, NIV)**

How do Christians Interpret Creation Differently?

There are various interpretations of the creation story among Christians.

I am a Creationist. I believe that Genesis is a **literal** account of how God created the world, and that it tells the story exactly as it happened.

I believe that the creation story is metaphorical. I think that the Bible describes **why** God created the world, but that science, including the Big Bang theory and evolution, explain **how**.

The Nature of God

Christianity is a **monotheistic** religion – it teaches that there is only one God.

Many attributes are given to God, including that He is immanent, benevolent and the creator of everything. Other attributes given to God are that He is:

Omnipotent

Christians believe that God is all-powerful and can do anything. Only an omnipotent God could possibly do the things stated in the Bible; one example of this is his role as creator of the world. God's omnipotence allows Him to help those in need, reward the worthy and punish the evil.

Loving

Christianity teaches that God loves his creations and wants what is best for them. Christians are encouraged to love others and treat them well. In the Bible, Jesus says the greatest commandment is to *'love your neighbour as yourself.'* **(Mark 12:31, NIV).**

Just

God is the ultimate judge. He judges people fairly based on their actions. A person's actions in life will determine whether they go to heaven or hell. Those who sin and do not follow God's laws will be punished. However, sinners will be forgiven if they are sorry.

The Trinity

Although Christianity teaches that there is only one God, most Christians believe that there are three distinct persons within this one God. This is the idea of the Trinity, which is outlined in the Nicene Creed; a statement of belief about the nature of God.

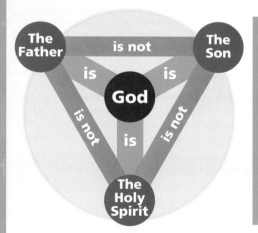

- **God the Father** – God the Father created Heaven, Earth and all living things.

- **God the Son** – God the Son is Jesus Christ. In His human form on Earth, He is both fully human and fully divine.

- **God the Holy Spirit** – God the Holy Spirit is God's presence on Earth. Once Jesus had left the Earth, the Holy Spirit came to guide, influence and sustain the world. Christians feel its presence in their daily lives.

The diagram of the Trinity is designed to show how each part of God is interlinked. Not all Christians believe in the Trinity; for example, Unitarians and Christadelphians.

Remember: The Trinity is the idea of one God with three distinct roles, not three different Gods!

The Problem of Evil and Suffering

The nature of God is often challenged by the existence of evil and suffering. There are two types of evil:

Moral evil

Human actions which are morally wrong and result in suffering, such as murder or theft.

Natural evil

Natural disasters that result in suffering, such as earthquakes or volcanoes.

Christianity teaches that evil and suffering are the result of **the Fall** – the moment Adam and Eve disobeyed God and ate the forbidden fruit from the Tree of Knowledge in the Garden of Eden.

God allowed humans to endure suffering as punishment for this **original sin**.

'...every inclination of the human heart is evil from childhood.' **(Genesis 8:21, NIV)**

The existence of evil and suffering causes some people to question their faith and the nature of God.

'Is God really <u>omnipotent</u> if evil and suffering exist?'

'Is God really <u>loving</u> if people are suffering and God doesn't seem to care?'

'Is God really <u>just</u> if He allows innocent people to endure terrible suffering?'

Christianity explains evil in three main ways:

1 Evil is a test from God. People must endure suffering yet remain faithful to God to show their love for Him. People can also react positively by following Jesus's example and helping those suffering.

2 God created humans in His own image, giving them free will so they could make their own decisions. People can choose to be good or evil; when they choose evil, suffering happens.

3 God works in mysterious ways and nobody can know his plans for humanity. God has His reasons for allowing evil and suffering, but Christians must accept this as part of His divine plan.

'And the God of all grace, who called you to his eternal glory in Christ, after you have suffered a little while, will himself restore you and make you strong, firm and steadfast.' **(Peter 5:10, NIV)**

Jesus Christ & Salvation

Incarnation and Jesus as the Son of God

The incarnation is the idea that God became flesh in the form of Jesus.

'The Word became flesh and made his dwelling among us. We have seen his glory, the glory of the one and only Son, who came from the Father, full of grace and truth.' **(John 1:14, NIV)**

Before his birth, Jesus's mother, Mary, was visited by the angel Gabriel. Gabriel told her:

'...you have found favor with God. You will conceive and give birth to a son, and you are to call him Jesus. He will be great and will be called the Son of the Most High. The Lord God will give him the throne of his father David...' **(Luke 1:30-32, NIV)**

Jesus is often called 'Christ' or 'Messiah', which translates to 'the anointed one'. The name Jesus also originates from 'Yeshua', which means 'salvation'; Jesus was sent to save people from sin and reunite them with God's love. Jesus was born both fully human and fully divine.

During his lifetime, Jesus carried out good deeds, spread the word of God and performed miracles.

Crucifixion

The Roman governor, Pontius Pilate, sentenced Jesus to death by crucifixion for claiming to be the Son of God. Jesus was severely beaten, nailed to a wooden cross through his hands and feet and left to die. One of the centurions who witnessed Jesus's humiliating and agonising death on the cross, proclaimed:

'Surely this man was the Son of God!' **(Mark 15:39, NIV)**

Whilst on the cross, Jesus forgave those who had wronged him. Jesus's willing sacrifice to save humanity is the foundation for all Christianity.

Resurrection

After his death, Jesus's body was placed in a tomb. However, when several women came one morning to anoint his body, they found the tomb empty. The stone covering it had rolled away.

Two men in shining robes asked the women:

'Why do you look for the living among the dead? He is not here; he has risen!' **(Luke 24:5-6, NIV)**

The resurrection of Jesus on Easter Sunday is seen as proof of his victory of life over death and assures Christians of the promise of eternal life.

daydream EDUCATION

Ascension

On the fortieth day after his resurrection, Jesus ascended into heaven. Before his ascension, Jesus spoke to his followers, instructing them to carry on his work and to spread the word of God:

'Go into all the world and preach the gospel to all creation. Whoever believes and is baptized will be saved...' **(Mark 16:15-16, NIV)**

The ascension of Jesus shows that there is a place for all Christians in heaven. Spreading the word of God and doing good deeds continues to be a duty for all Christians today.

Salvation

Sins are actions or thoughts that separate people from God. Many Christians believe that everyone is born with the ability to sin as a result of **The Original Sin** (Adam's disobedience of God's command not to eat the fruit from the Tree of Knowledge).

Salvation is the saving of the soul from sin and death, leading to a life in heaven. Salvation is gained through:

Law

This includes following Jesus's example as well as the Bible's teachings (such as the laws of the **Ten Commandments**) in order to live a good life.

Grace

This means being saved by Jesus's sacrifice. Grace is not earned but is a gift from God.

Spirit

Christians believe that the Holy Spirit guides them to live a good life and follow the teachings of their faith.

Atonement

Atonement is the reconciliation of God and mankind through Jesus Christ. Jesus died on the cross to win forgiveness from God for the sins of mankind. It was a powerful act of love, where God gave up his only son to save others.

"'He himself bore our sins' in his body on the cross, so that we might die to sins and live for righteousness; 'by his wounds you have been healed.'"
(1 Peter 2:24, NIV)

The Afterlife

Christians believe in the afterlife and the concept of a soul (the non-physical spiritual part of a human being), which lives on after death.

Resurrection and Judgement

The resurrection of Jesus after his crucifixion gives Christians hope for eternal life.

"Jesus said to her, 'I am the resurrection and the life. The one who believes in me will live, even though they die; and whoever lives by believing in me will never die. Do you believe this?'" **(John 11:25-26, NIV)**

Some Christians believe that the afterlife will begin as soon as they die, whereas others expect a Day of Judgement when Jesus will return, resurrect the dead and decide their fate.

The Bible makes it very clear that people will be judged by God on how they lived their lives. God will reward those who are worthy with heaven, and those who are not will be punished in hell.

'...they will go away to eternal punishment, but the righteous to eternal life.' **(Matthew 25:46, NIV)**

Heaven and Hell

There are several references to heaven and hell in the bible:

'For we know that if the earthly tent (body) we live in is destroyed, we have a building from God, an eternal house in heaven, not built by human hands.'

(2 Corinthians 5:1, NIV)

'Whoever believes in the Son has eternal life, but whoever rejects the Son will not see life, but God's wrath remains on them.'

(John 3:36, NIV)

Some Christians believe that heaven is a physical place of paradise where people can live happily in the presence of God and their loved ones for eternity, and hell is a physical place of eternal torture and misery, ruled over by the Devil.

Others believe that heaven and hell are states of mind – heaven is a state of being united with God and hell is separation from God for eternity. Hell could also mean **annihilation** (destruction) of the soul.

Purgatory

Roman Catholics believe that after death, souls that are not entirely free from sin but are ultimately destined for heaven are held in a temporary state, place or condition of punishment, known as purgatory.

According to the catechism of the Catholic Church, during purgatory, the soul undergoes purification so that it can *'achieve the holiness necessary to enter the joy of heaven'*.

daydream EDUCATION

Christian Faith in Action

The Role of the Church in the Local Community

The church is primarily a place for Christians to meet and worship, but it also has a key role in the wider community. It brings people together and creates a sense of belonging for those involved.

> *'And let us consider how we may spur one another on toward love and good deeds, not giving up meeting together...but encouraging one another...'* **(Hebrews 10:24-25, NIV)**

Christianity teaches that **salvation** can be achieved through following Jesus's example and helping others. Churches work to unite and help people in the community in the following ways:

Running youth clubs

Running food banks to feed those in poverty

Running Bible study groups and Sunday schools

Hosting coffee mornings

Fundraising for charity

Sending out Street Pastors to keep people safe at night

Providing rites of passage (e.g. baptisms, weddings)

Visiting people in prison or hospital

Ecumenism works to unite different denominations as one community of Christians. Some churches will hold joint services, work on community projects or host events to bring groups together.

Evangelism

Evangelism means spreading the teachings of Jesus through the 'good news' (the Gospels). Some Christians believe they should actively convert people to their faith:

"He said to them, 'Go into all the world and preach the gospel to all creation.'"
(Mark 16:15, NIV)

The aim of this is to unite others through Christianity and spread the message of salvation. There are two main ways people can do this:

Church Growth

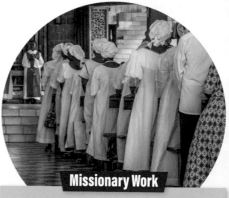

Missionary Work

Evangelism is more important than ever in the UK's changing society; between 1983 and 2015, the proportion of Christians in Britain fell from 55% to 43% (however, it is important to note that worldwide it is a rapidly growing religion).

Some Christians spread their faith through knocking on doors, street preaching or through initiatives such as the **Alpha course** (a series of talks exploring Christianity).

Some Christians choose to spread the Christian message abroad through missionary work. For example, organisations such as **The Evangelical Alliance Mission (TEAM)** 'help churches send missionaries to establish reproducing churches in other nations to the glory of God'.

They work to improve healthcare, education and community development, as well as provide disaster aid to people in need.

Remember: Not all evangelists talk directly about their faith. Some groups, such as the Salvation Army, demonstrate **agape** (love) by helping the needy in the community.

daydream EDUCATION

The Worldwide Church

Christianity is made up of many denominations, but these are all united by the worldwide Church.

Reconciliation

> *'Be kind and compassionate to one another, forgiving each other, just as in Christ God forgave you.'* (Ephesians 4:32, NIV)

Christians are taught to always work towards **reconciliation** (bringing people together for a peaceful resolution). Jesus sacrificed himself to bring about reconciliation between God and mankind. It is therefore important to follow his example so that sins can be forgiven.

Within the Christian Church, the existence of various denominations has sometimes caused conflict. Despite this, one of the guiding principles of the Church is to work towards peace.

The Fellowship of Reconciliation (FoR) is a Christian organisation which promotes non-violence through the teachings of Jesus as a radical peacemaker. Some of its work involves championing disarmament, focusing particularly on nuclear weapons and armed drones.

Persecution

Persecution is ill-treatment of others, usually because of race or political or religious beliefs. Despite a commitment to peace and reconciliation, in 2017 the International Society for Human Rights claimed that 80% of all acts of religious persecution were directed at Christians.

In some cases, Christians have been imprisoned, attacked or even killed for their beliefs.

Christian Solidarity Worldwide is one of the many Church campaign groups which help persecuted Christians. It works to raise awareness of religious persecution, influence governments, train people in human rights laws and help the oppressed to speak up.

Christian Charities

Christians are taught to follow the example of Jesus by helping those in need. Parables such as the Good Samaritan (**Luke 10:25-37**) teach that Christians can only enter the Kingdom of Heaven if they show love to others; in other words, *'love thy neighbour'*.

Charity is one of the ways in which Christians can show love by helping others.

Christian Aid

This is the official relief agency for 41 Church denominations across the UK and Ireland. It works to relieve global poverty by providing food, aid, shelter, sanitation and water to those in need.

CAFOD

This is the official aid agency of the Catholic Church in England and Wales. It works to improve access to clean water, education and healthcare. It also fights for workers' rights, safe working conditions and fair pay.

Tearfund

This is an evangelical organisation that travels to disaster areas to help ease poverty and provide support for refugees. Tearfund also works to help develop communities, envision churches and influence local, national and international policies.

15

Worship and Prayer

Worship

Christians worship to show their appreciation of God and express their love and devotion to him. Christians may worship alone (private worship) or as part of a group in their place of worship (public worship). It can involve prayers, hymns, celebrating festivals, and pilgrimage, but can also include good deeds and music. Different denominations have different ideas about worship.

Liturgical Worship

Christian liturgy is a pattern of worship that is used by many Christian denominations on a regular basis. It includes prayers, hymns and readings from the Bible and the Book of Common Prayer. Worship is generally based around the sacraments and Holy Communion.

Liturgical worship is part of a long-standing tradition and can therefore be found in churches all over the world, helping Christians to feel part of the wider church community.

Liturgical worship is used in Anglican, Catholic and Orthodox churches.

Non-Liturgical Worship

Non-liturgical worship is less formal and does not follow a strict or regular pattern. Although the basic structure may remain the same, the priest may change the order and the service may vary each time. Worship is often focused on Bible readings, sermons, prayers and music.

Some Christians believe that non-liturgical worship offers a more personal experience, allowing them to express their love and devotion to God in a more relevant and connected way.

Methodist and Pentecostal worship is usually non-liturgical.

Informal Worship

Informal worship ceremonies are often based on spontaneous prayers and sharing of thoughts. It may also include singing, clapping and 'speaking in tongues' (unknown languages).

Christians who take part in informal worship believe it is similar to the early forms of worship that were practised before the Church became more structured. It is arguably the most personal form of public worship, allowing people to share their feelings about their faith with others.

Informal worship is popular with Evangelists.

Private Worship

Private worship allows Christians to form a personal relationship with God and usually takes place within the home. It can include singing hymns, praying, or reading the Bible. Private worship can help people feel close to God whenever they wish.

'But when you pray, go into your room, close the door and pray to your Father, who is unseen. Then your Father, who sees what is done in secret, will reward you.' (Matthew 6:6, NIV)

daydream
EDUCATION

Prayer

Christians communicate with God through prayer. They believe that God hears all of their prayers, whether these are silent or spoken aloud. Some choose to use formal, set prayers, whereas others opt for more personal, informal prayer.

Set Prayers

These are formal, set prayers usually found in prayer books and used in church worship.

Informal Prayer

Informal prayer is a personal communication with God.

Different forms of prayer include:

Adoration
Expressing great love and praise for God

Confession
Admitting sins to God in order to seek forgiveness

Thanksgiving
Thanking God

Supplication
Asking God for something

Intercession
Asking God to help somebody else

Christians believe that God will answer their prayers, though this may not always be in the way they want or expect. During prayer, they listen carefully for God's answers. Prayer can help Christians develop a relationship with God and comfort them during times of suffering.

The Lord's Prayer

The Lord's Prayer is the most well-known Christian prayer. It was said to be the prayer which Jesus taught to his followers and reveals teachings about God.

The Lord's Prayer shows that:

God is the Father in heaven – This links to the Christian idea of heaven in the afterlife and God's roles in the Trinity.

God's will shall be done – This refers to the Kingdom of God on earth in the gospels of St Mark.

God is forgiving – This is an important link to salvation and shows Christians that they should also forgive.

Our Father, who art in heaven,
hallowed be thy name;
thy kingdom come;
thy will be done
on earth as it is in heaven.
Give us this day our daily bread
and forgive us our trespasses
as we forgive those who
trespass against us
and lead us not into temptation,
but deliver us from evil.
For thine is the kingdom,
the power, and the glory,
for ever and ever.
Amen.

Remember: All forms of worship/prayer have their positives and negatives. You should explore these in detail if the exam question asks.

The Sacraments

A sacrament is a religious ceremony or ritual. It is administered by the Church and helps Christians to receive God's grace, strengthening their relationship with Him.

Beliefs about the sacraments vary between different denominations. Roman Catholic and Orthodox Christians believe that there are seven sacraments, whereas Protestants generally believe that Jesus only prescribed two sacraments: baptism and the Eucharist.

Some Christian groups, such as Quakers, think that sacraments are not needed to be close to God.

Baptism

The sacrament of baptism is used to admit people into the Christian faith. Through baptism, the recipients acknowledge Jesus Christ as their saviour and dedicate their life to God. At this point they receive God's grace, where they are cleansed of the original sin.

'Therefore go and make disciples of all nations, baptizing them in the name the Father and of the Son and of the Holy Spirit...' **(Matthew 28:19, NIV)**

Baptism was part of the **Great Commission**: Jesus's command to recruit new disciples into Christianity. This teaching has encouraged people to take up the mission and become Evangelists.

Infant Baptism

Many Christians perform infant baptisms. The sign of the cross is made on the baby and water is poured three times over the head to represent the Trinity. In Orthodox Christianity, babies are fully immersed in the water.

Believer's Baptism

Some Christians, such as Baptists and Pentecostals, believe that a person should make their own choice to become a Christian when they are old enough. Believers are immersed in water, just as John did in the Bible.

Denominations that have infant baptisms often hold a confirmation ceremony when the child is old enough, allowing them to declare (or confirm) their belief in God and Jesus.

Holy Communion (The Eucharist)

The Eucharist is a service in which Christians commemorate Jesus's sacrifice to save mankind from sin. They remember the Last Supper, where Jesus promised his followers that he would always be with them. He shared bread and wine, declaring:

'Drink from it, all of you. This is my blood of the covenant, which is poured out for many for the forgiveness of sins. I tell you, I will not drink from this fruit of the vine from now on until the day when I drink it new with you in my Father's kingdom.' **(Mark 26:27-29, NIV)**

Some Christians, such as Roman Catholics, believe in transubstantiation; the literal conversion of wine and bread into the blood and flesh of Jesus during Mass. Others, such as Baptists, believe that the transformation is more symbolic and represents God's presence.

The Eucharist can be carried out in a variety of ways depending on the denomination or tradition, but the sharing of the bread and wine remains a constant theme.

The Seven Catholic Sacraments

In Catholic Christianity, there are seven sacraments.

1

Baptism

Baptism allows people to officially join the Church.

2

Confirmation

Once old enough (usually when they become teenagers), Christians will reaffirm their commitment to the Christian faith. This is important, as they are now old enough to fully understand the promise being made. Sometimes the bishop places their hands on a person's head or anoints them with oil (**chrism**).

3

Reconciliation

Reconciliation (formerly known as **confession**) involves confessing and showing repentance for sins. In response to a confession, a priest will then give a **penance**, a certain action that must be carried out in order to receive **absolution** (God's forgiveness).

4

Anointing the Sick

Also known as extreme unction or the last rites, anointing the sick is performed when a priest or bishop anoints a sick person with the 'oil of the sick'. This is done to help renew the person's spiritual strength and help them cope with the suffering and hardship of serious illness. It is believed that sometimes miraculous healing can occur, but only at God's will.

5

Matrimony

Jesus was believed to have performed his first miracle at a wedding. Catholic Christians therefore see weddings as having special spiritual significance; they believe that God is personally present at the ceremony to see the couple establish a lifelong partnership.

6

Holy Orders

Those who seek a spiritual life, such as priests, bishops and deacons, take up holy orders to serve God. This is treated as a lifelong commitment.

7

The Eucharist

This is known to Catholics as Mass and is the ceremony where transubstantiation happens: people join together to receive the body and blood of Christ. It is seen as an act of liturgical worship, where people share their faith as a community.

daydream EDUCATION

Pilgrimage & Festivals

Although not compulsory in Christianity, some Christians choose to go on a **pilgrimage** (journey of spiritual importance) to show their devotion to God. Other reasons for pilgrimage include:

To seek healing

To feel closer to God

To visit places important to their faith

To seek forgiveness

To seek God's guidance in difficult times

To learn from the example of other pilgrims

Some Christians feel pilgrimage is unnecessary and prefer to focus on their faith more personally.

Christian Sites of Pilgrimage

Christians often visit sites that were key to Jesus's life, such as Jerusalem, or go to peaceful places which allow time for focusing on faith.

Popular sites of pilgrimage include:

Iona

Iona is an island just off the west coast of Scotland and was where St Columba brought Christianity to Scotland in the 6th century. Christians often travel here in dedication to the Virgin Mary and to spend time in prayer. The Iona community also hold daily services and a weekly 'pilgrimage walk' to visit the island's holy and historical spots.

Lourdes

Many Christians visit the small village of Lourdes in the south of France as they believe that it has been the location of many miracles. In the 19th century, a young girl named Bernadette had several visions of the Virgin Mary. During one vision, Mary told her to drink from the waters of the spring they were standing at; people today still visit these waters for their healing powers.

The Vatican (Rome)

The Vatican is home of the Pope, the leader of the Roman Catholic Church. It has symbolic and spiritual significance for visiting pilgrims, bringing them close to their spiritual leader and helping them to feel part of the wider Christian community.

Lindisfarne (Holy Island)

Lindisfarne is an island just off the north-east coast of England and is where the early Christians founded Lindisfarne Monastery in 635 AD. It is a special place of pilgrimage for Christians, as it is where the Lindisfarne Gospels were written. These make up a beautiful and intricately-detailed handwritten copy of the Holy Bible.

Festivals

There are many special celebrations in the Christian calendar, but the two most important are Christmas and Easter, which mark the birth and death of Jesus Christ.

Christmas

Christmas is the annual festival commemorating the birth of Jesus. It is celebrated by most Christians on 25th December. Traditional Christian customs associated with Christmas include:

Advent

This begins four Sundays before Christmas and is a time of preparation, prayer and reflection. People often light Advent candles or open Advent calendars to count down to Christmas Day.

Gifts and Cards

People exchange gifts to represent the idea of Jesus being a gift to the world from God. They also send Christmas cards, often depicting religious scenes.

Nativity Plays

Nativity plays are usually performed in schools where all the children get involved, acting out the events of Jesus's birth in Bethlehem.

Most Christian denominations hold a special 'Midnight Mass' on Christmas Eve to mark the start of the life of Jesus and remember how his life would lead to the salvation of all Christians.

'For to us, a child is born, to us a son is given, and the government will be on his shoulders. And he will be called Wonderful Counselor, Mighty God, Everlasting Father, Prince of Peace.' **(Isaiah 9:6, NIV)**

Easter

During Easter, Christians remember how Jesus died for their sins and then rose again, defeating death through his resurrection.

Easter is the most important festival for Christians as it celebrates Jesus's sacrifice for mankind. It is proof to Christians of Jesus's role as the Messiah and reminds them of the eternal life promised to them for believing in him. The key events of Easter include:

Lent	The 40-day period of fasting and reflection before Easter, starting on Ash Wednesday. During this time, Christians remember Jesus's time in the desert, where he fasted for 40 days.
Palm Sunday	The Sunday before Easter marks the beginning of Holy Week and Jesus's arrival into Jerusalem where crowds placed palm leaves on the floor and cheered.
Holy Wednesday	This is sometimes known as 'Spy Wednesday', when Christians remember the deal struck by Judas to betray Jesus.
Maundy Thursday	Christians remember the Last Supper, which Jesus shared with his disciples on the night before he died.
Good Friday	This marks the day Jesus was crucified; the term 'good' reflects how his sacrifice brought about salvation and proved he was the Messiah.
Easter Sunday	This is a celebration of the resurrection of Jesus following his crucifixion. Christians mark the occasion by attending church services and lighting the Paschal candle, which reminds them that Jesus is the Light of the World.

I am a Muslim

Islam is the religion of Muslims. Muslims believe in Allah and his prophet, Muhammad.

God

I believe that there is only one God, Allah, and that Muhammad was the last prophet sent by Allah.

Holy Book

The imam instructs me from the Qur'an in Arabic. The Qur'an was revealed to the Prophet Muhammad by God. It teaches me how to worship Allah and how to behave towards others.

Muslim Festivals

Ramadan: The holy month during which Muslims fast from sunrise to sunset.

Id-ul-Fitr: A celebration to mark the end of Ramadan.

Id-ul-Adha: A celebration of Ibrahim's willingness to sacrifice his son to God.

Worship

I pray five times a day, facing Makkah (Mecca), at home or in the mosque. I wash before praying and use a prayer mat. When entering the Mosque, I take off my shoes. Women and men do not pray in the same area of the mosque.

Dietary Customs

I am allowed to eat halal food. Some foods, such as pork, are forbidden, and all food must be prepared in a certain way.

Five Pillars of Islam

Every Muslim must follow the Five Pillars of Islam.

Shahadah: declaration of faith

Salah: praying five times a day

Zakah: giving money to charity/alms

Sawm: fasting during Ramadan

Hajj: pilgrimage to Makkah

Jihad

As well as following the Five Pillars of Islam, I must understand jihad and strive to be a good Muslim. Greater jihad is the personal struggle to live a life of obedience to God and to not give in to temptation. Lesser jihad is the physical struggle to protect the Islamic faith in the world.

daydream EDUCATION

Sunni & Shi'a Islam

 Sunni and **Shi'a** are the two main branches within Islam. It is estimated that 85–90% of Muslims are Sunni Muslims, and 10–15% are Shi'a Muslims.

The Sunni and Shi'a Divide

After the death of Muhammad in 632 CE, a period of conflict ensued. Abu Bakr was appointed as caliph (leader) of Islam, but some Muslims rejected this, believing that Muhammad designated his cousin and son-in-law, Ali, as his successor.

Ali eventually became the fourth caliph. However, after his death, Islam split with Shi'a Muslims believing that caliphs should be descendants of Muhammad and Sunni Muslims believing that the caliph should be chosen by the community.

The Six Articles of Faith (Sunni Islam)

There are six articles of faith in Sunni Islam.

1	Tawhid	Allah is the one and only God.
2	Angels (Malaikah)	Angels are messengers sent to the prophets by Allah.
3	The Holy Books	The holy books are the word of Allah and are the highest authority in Islam. The Qur'an is the main book of Islam.
4	Prophets (Nubuwwah)	The prophets are the proclaimers of Allah's will.
5	The Day of Judgement	All humanity will be judged by Allah after death.
6	The Supremacy of God's Will (al-Qadr)	Allah knows about, and controls, everything that happens.

The Five Roots of Usul ad-Din (Shi'a Islam)

The five roots of faith in Shi'a Islam are known as Usul ad-Din.

1	Tawhid	Allah is the one and only God.
2	Divine Justice (Adl)	Allah is just and wise. He is fair in his treatment.
3	Prophethood (Nubuwwah)	The prophets are the proclaimers of Allah's will.
4	The Imamate (Imamah)	Imams are the leaders of Islam and protect the truth of the religion. They are the successors to Muhammad.
5	The Resurrection (Ma'ad)	After death, humans will be resurrected and judged by God.

Shi'a Islam is divided into further sub-branches. The three main ones are **Twelvers** (*Ithna `Asharis*), **Seveners** (*Isma`ilis*), and **Fivers** (*Zaydis*), each believing in a different line of imams.

Remember: The articles of faith differ slightly between Sunni and Shi'a Islam, but they both agree on the fundamentals of the faith and share the same holy book, the Qur'an.

23

The Nature of Allah

Islam is a monotheistic religion, which means that Muslims believe in only one God – Allah.

Tawhid: The Oneness of God

Tawhid means 'oneness' and is the main focus of the **Shahadah** (the Muslim profession of faith).

'He is God, [who is] One, God, the Eternal Refuge. He neither begets nor is born, Nor is there to Him any equivalent.' **(Surah 112)**

Islam teaches that nothing and no one can compare to Allah, and that Allah is the only god. Therefore, it prohibits images or idols of Allah, as this would endorse the worst possible sin: the sin of **shirk** (deification or worship of anyone or anything besides Allah).

The Nature of Allah

Islam teaches that Allah is the creator of the world and everything in it. For Muslims, Allah is the greatest and all others are beneath him; the very word 'Islam' means submission (Muslims submit themselves to the will of one almighty God).

The nature of Allah is revealed in the holy book, the Qur'an. Allah is:

Immanent	Transcendent	Omnipotent
Allah is present in the world and involved in the lives of humans.	Allah is outside of existence and beyond human understanding.	Allah is an all-powerful creator and has control over everything.
Beneficent	**Merciful**	**Just**
Allah is all-loving, good and kind.	Allah shows compassion and forgiveness.	Allah treats all fairly. The Justice of Allah is known as Adalat in Shi'a Islam.

There are 99 names for Allah listed in the Qur'an, all of which give an indication of Allah's attributes; for example, **Al-Rahman** (the Compassionate) and **Al-Adl** (the Just).

Muslims may pray using a string of 99 beads, known as a **misbaha**. They are used as a guide during prayer to help them remember the 99 names of Allah.

Angels (Malaikah)

In Islam, angels (also known as **malaikah**) are the *'honoured servants'* **(Surah 21:26)** of Allah. Muslims believe that these supernatural beings were the first creations of Allah and that they pass the word of Allah to prophets. Angels have no free will and are therefore free of sin. They exist only to serve and obey Allah and can take no action unless commanded first:

'...they do not disobey God in what He commands them but do what they are commanded.' **(Surah 66:6)**

Angels are described in the Qur'an as being made from light and having wings. Part of their role is to act as guardians and to record the deeds of humans ready for the Day of Judgement.

Jibril (Gabriel)

Jibril, the **Angel of Revelation**, is a trusted messenger of Allah. He revealed the words of the Qur'an to Muhammad and was the angel entrusted to tell Maryam (Mary) that she was pregnant with Isa (Jesus). Jibril also revealed messages to the prophets.

Mika'il (Michael)

Mika'il, the **Angel of Mercy**, is responsible for rewarding the righteous and punishing the bad. Mika'il also asks Allah to forgive the sins of those who seek to be forgiven.

Belief in angels is one of the **six articles of faith** in Sunni Islam.

Prophethood (Risalah)

The belief that Allah chose prophets (humans) to deliver the message of Islam to the rest of mankind is known as **Risalah**.

Despite the Qur'an mentioning only 25 messengers, most Muslims believe that Allah chose 124,000 messengers to deliver the message of the oneness of God and how to lead a good life.

Adam

Father of humans, Adam, was the first man, first Muslim and first prophet of Islam. He and his wife, Hawa (Eve), lived happily in the Garden of Bliss until they disobeyed God by eating fruit from a forbidden tree.

Allah forgave Adam for his sin, but banished him to Earth, where he would deliver the message of Islam to others and teach them how to live a good life.

Ibrahim (Abraham)

Muslims believe Ibrahim fulfilled all of the tests that Allah set for him, including His request to sacrifice his own son (which Allah then stopped; He simply wanted to test Ibrahim's faith).

He also campaigned against the worship of false idols. Today, the festival of **Id-ul-Adha** commemorates Ibrahim's willingness to sacrifice his son.

Muhammad

Born in Makkah (Mecca), Saudi Arabia, Muhammad is believed to have been the last prophet of Allah: 'the Seal of the Prophets'.

Whilst meditating in a cave near Mecca, Muhammad received his first revelation from the angel Jibril (Gabriel). During the revelation, Jibril is believed to have ordered Muhammad to recite a verse. After this point, Jibril revealed the Qur'an (Word of God) to Muhammad over a period of approximately 23 years.

Believing that God had chosen him as his messenger, Muhammad spent his life preaching the oneness of god and encouraging Muslims to lead a good life.

The Holy Books

The Qur'an is considered the most important Islamic text and is seen by Muslims as the literal word of God.

Revealed to the Prophet Muhammad through the angel Jibril over a period of 23 years, the Qur'an consists of 114 surahs (chapters) made up of ayahs (verses).

The word Qur'an means 'recitation'; it was revealed to Muhammad verbally because he could not read or write. His followers wrote down what he told them.

The Qur'an teaches Muslims how to live good lives in order to please Allah. They learn the text in its original Arabic so that the meaning does not become lost in translation.

We always treat the Qur'an with great respect when we worship. We keep it wrapped up carefully on a high shelf, wash our hands before touching it and place it on a special stand when reading.

A Muslim who has memorised and can recite the Qur'an off by heart is known as a **Hafiz**.

Other Holy Books in Islam

The Tawrat (Torah)
Allah revealed the Tawrat to the Prophet Musa (Moses). The Tawrat is an important holy book in Islam. However, Muslims believe that it has been altered and is therefore not completely reliable.

The Zabur (Psalms)
Allah revealed the Zabur to the Prophet Dawud (David). Muslims believe that the Zabur is similar to the Psalms in the Bible. However, like the Tawrat, Muslims believe that the Zabur has been corrupted.

The Sahifa (Scrolls of Abraham)
This was the first holy book and was said to have been revealed by Allah to the Prophet Ibrahim (Abraham). The Sahifa is now lost.

The Injil (Gospel)
Allah revealed the Injil (gospel) to the Prophet Isa (Jesus). Many Muslims believe that the Injil contains prophecies about the coming of Muhammad. However, they also believe that it has become distorted and corrupt over time.

Muslims also look to the Hadith (the written record of Muhammad's words and teachings) for guidance, as well as the Sunnah, which reveals Muhammad's way of life according to the Hadith. Though these are important, it is the Qur'an which has ultimate authority.

daydream EDUCATION

Life After Death

In Islam, the afterlife is known as Akhirah. It is an important part of the Islamic faith. Life is a test for each individual for the afterlife.

Al-Qadr (Predestination)

Some Muslims believe that everything is predetermined (planned) by the will of Allah. This is known as al-Qadr. The amount of free will that Muslims believe Allah has given them varies between different branches of Islam.

Sunni Muslims place more emphasis on the idea that Allah already knows everything that is going to happen. They believe that humans have free will, but that Allah has already set out the choices they are going to make.

Shi'a Muslims are more inclined towards the idea of humans having free will. Although they believe that Allah is all-knowing and must therefore know what is going to happen, it is up to humans to make their own decisions.

"And never say of anything, 'Indeed, I will do that tomorrow,' Except, [when adding], 'If God wills.' And remember your Lord when you forget [it] and say, 'Perhaps my Lord will guide me to what is nearer than this to right conduct.'" **(Surah 18:23-24)**

Yawm ad-Din (The Day Of Judgement)

Yawm ad-Din is the Day of Judgement, the end of time, when all human beings will be resurrected (raised from the dead) and judged by God for their deeds.

Good intentions and actions will be rewarded. Bad actions will be punished, but bad intentions will not be punished as long as they are not acted upon.

The concept of Yawm ad-Din encourages Muslims to lead good lives.

Jannah

Those who perform good deeds and have faith in Allah are rewarded with life in paradise (Jannah).

Jannah is described in the Qur'an as a paradise where *'...gardens beneath which rivers flow, wherein they abide eternally, and pleasant dwellings in gardens of perpetual residence...'* **(Surah 9:72)**

Jahannam

Those who reject Allah and do evil will be punished with a life in hell (Jahannam), a place of fire and great torment.

'Indeed, those who disbelieve and die while they are disbelievers – upon them will be the curse of God and of the angels and the people, all together, Abiding eternally therein. The punishment will not be lightened for them, nor will they be reprieved.' **(Surah 2:161-162)**

The **barzakh** mentioned in the Qur'an is a barrier which separates the physical world from the spiritual. Muslims believe that this is where people's souls will remain in waiting until the call of the angel Israfil signals the beginning of **Yawm ad-Din**.

27

The Five Pillars of Islam

| Shahadah | Salah | Zakah | Sawm | Hajj |

It is a duty for all Muslims to follow the five pillars of Islam. Observing each pillar is an act of **ibadah**, or worship. The pillars keep Muslims in close contact with Allah, and show moral and spiritual discipline, solidarity, equality and brotherhood (ummah). Sunni Muslims believe in the Five Pillars of Islam. Four of the Five Pillars are also included in the Ten Obligatory Acts for Shi'a Muslims.

Shahadah - Declaration of Faith

'There is no deity but God. Muhammad is the messenger of God.'

The Shahadah is the declaration of faith for all Muslims and demonstrates loyalty to Allah and the Prophet Muhammad. It is recited to new-born babies at birth and to the dying to demonstrate a commitment to Islam. Muslims must recite this several times each day to remind them of Allah and their faith.

Some Shi'a Muslims add *'and Ali is the wali of God'* but it is not obligatory.

Salah - Prayer

Muslims must pray five times a day: between dawn and sunrise (**Fajr**), noon (**Zuhr**), late afternoon (**Asr**), after sunset (**Maghrib**) and nightfall (**Isha**).

Ritual washing (wudu) is performed before salah to purify the body and mind. During wudu, Muslims state their intentions (niyyah) to pray and will focus solely on Allah.

All Muslims face the holy city of Makkah during prayer. Men and women pray separately to avoid distraction. Men are required to go to Friday prayers (Jummah) at the mosque. Praying at the mosque increases the Muslim sense of community (**ummah**). Prayer positions (rak'ah) ensure that Muslims show total submission to Allah.

Rak'ah is the set pattern of movements followed during prayer. During prayer, Muslims recite the first chapter of the Qur'an as well as other verses. **'Allahu Akbar'** (God is great) is also repeated several times during a rak'ah. To end prayer, Muslims face right and then left and say **'Assalamu alaikum wa rahmatullah'** (Peace be upon you, and the mercy and blessings of Allah).

daydream EDUCATION

Zakah – Almsgiving

Muslims are obliged to contribute 2.5% of residual annual savings to help the Muslim community. This teaches Muslims to share and be less materialistic. The act of giving zakah means purifying one's wealth to gain Allah's blessing to make it grow in goodness. Wealth is given by Allah, so it should be used to serve Allah.

'Never will you attain the good [reward] until you spend [in the way of God] from that which you love. And whatever you spend – indeed, God is Knowing of it.' **(Surah 3:92)**

Some Shi'a Muslims also pay khums (20% of surplus income) in addition to zakah.

Sawm – Fasting

Muslims must fast through daylight hours during the month of Ramadan and engage in increased prayer and charity. Muslims look forward to sawm even though it requires hardship. It is a time when their faith is tested, a time to learn compassion, empathy, patience, tolerance, self-discipline and obedience to Allah.

'And eat and drink until the white thread of dawn becomes distinct to you from the black thread [of night]. Then complete the fast until the night [i.e., sunset].' **(Surah 2:187)**

It is forbidden (haram) to drink, eat, smoke, have sexual intercourse, or purposely vomit during sawm. Some Muslims, such as the sick, children under the age of 12 and pregnant women, are not expected to fast.

Muslims believe that the angel Jibril revealed part of the Qur'an to the Prophet Muhammad during Ramadan. This event is known as **Laylat al-Qadr** (Night of Power) and is considered the holiest night of the year. The end of Ramadan is also the start of the festival of Id-ul-Fitr.

Hajj – Pilgrimage

Muslims must perform at least one pilgrimage to Makkah during Dhul Hijjah (the 12th Islamic month). Hajj consists of several ceremonies that symbolise the main beliefs of the Islamic faith and commemorate the trials of the Prophet Ibrahim and his family. It enables Muslims to come together to worship the One God.

8th Dhul Hijjah

Pilgrims perform:
- **Wudu** and wear ihram clothing
- **Tawaf** - circling the Kaaba (the holiest place in Islam) seven times anticlockwise
- **Sa'y** - travelling seven times between the hills of Safa and Marwah

9th Dhul Hijjah

Pilgrims visit Mount Arafat and spend the day in prayer asking for God's forgiveness and making promises to be better Muslims.

Mount Arafat is where Allah forgave Adam and Eve for their sins.

10th Dhul Hijjah

Pilgrims go to Mina to throw stones at three pillars that represent Shaytan (the Devil).

The Festival of Sacrifice, Id-ul-Adha, starts. Animals are sacrificed to remember the story of Ibrahim and Ishmael. Hair will also be shaved or cut.

11th - 12th Dhul Hijjah

Pilgrims stay at Mina and stone the pillars. They also return to the Kaaba to perform Tawaf.

Once the pilgrimage is complete, each pilgrim is given the title 'Hajji'.

Some believe that Hajj cleanses Hajjis of sin.

29

The Ten Obligatory Acts

There are ten duties that must be carried out by Shi'a Muslims, four of which are part of the **Five Pillars of Islam** (salah, sawm, zakah and hajj).

Salah

This is the ritual of prayer. Shi'a Muslims combine some prayers, so they pray three times a day rather than five. They also place their heads on a clay or wooden tablet (turbah) when worshipping.

Sawm

This is the ritual of fasting. Shi'a Muslims fast until after the last of the sunset has disappeared and night has fallen, whereas Sunni Muslims will only fast until the start of the sunset.

Zakah

This is 'almsgiving', where Muslims give 2.5% of their residual income to charity. Shi'a Muslims are very specific on what zakah can be used on: wheat, barley, dates, dried grapes, cows, camels, sheep, goats, gold and silver.

Hajj

This is the pilgrimage that Muslims must make, if they are able to, at least once in their lifetime. It should be done in the 12th Islamic month, Dhul Hijjah.

Khums

This is a 20% tax on any surplus income (or profit) earned. Khums is paid to those in need in the Islamic faith and to support Islamic education.

There are an additional six obligatory acts for Shi'a Muslims.

Jihad

This means to 'struggle' or 'strive'. Greater jihad is the personal struggle to live a life of obedience to Allah and to not give in to temptation. Lesser jihad is the physical struggle to protect the Islamic faith in the world.

Amr-bil-Maruf

This is the instruction to Muslims on how they should behave. It emphasises the importance of righteous actions and behaviour.

Nahi Anil Munkar

This is taught alongside amr-bil-maruf: 'Amr-bil-Maruf wa Nahi Anil Munkar' (enjoining good and forbidding evil). It discourages sinful behaviour.

Tawallah

This is the expression of love towards all that is good and those that follow Allah. Muslims see the lives of the prophets as perfect examples of this.

Tabarra

This is taught alongside tawalla and means to stay away from all that is evil and to dissociate themselves from the enemies of Allah.

daydream
EDUCATION

Jihad

Jihad means 'to struggle' or 'to strive' and is an obligation for all Muslims. There are two types:

Greater Jihad

Greater jihad is the personal struggle to follow Allah, resist temptation and carry out the duties required to lead a good Muslim life.

A good Muslim life involves studying the Qur'an, helping others, following the Five Pillars, and resisting temptation and greed.

Many Muslims believe that greater jihad is the most important of the two types and that the Prophet Muhammad shared this view.

Lesser Jihad

This is the struggle to protect the Islamic faith. Its aim is to improve the world and build a good Muslim society. This can be done through peaceful means; war is seen as a last resort.

In cases where conflict is deemed necessary, it can only be justified under certain conditions:

- It must only be fought in defence
- Civilians must not be harmed
- Holy buildings must not be damaged

'Permission [to fight] has been given to those who are being fought, because they were wronged.' (Surah 22:39)

Some extremists use lesser jihad as justification for terrorism. The vast majority of Muslims argue that this goes completely against the rules of jihad and would never condone terrorist actions.

Festivals

There are a number of important Islamic festivals that Muslims celebrate throughout the year.

Id-ul-Adha

Id-ul-Adha, the **'Festival of Sacrifice'**, takes place at the end of Hajj. It celebrates the Prophet Ibrahim's willingness to sacrifice his own son, Isma'il, to show his loyalty to Islam.

Ibrahim had a dream in which Allah told him to sacrifice his beloved son, so he took Isma'il to Mount Arafat where he told him about what Allah had instructed him to do. Isma'il understood but told Ibrahim to blindfold himself so that he wouldn't have to witness the sacrifice.

Ibrahim did as Allah had asked, but when he removed his blindfold, to his surprise, he saw the body of a dead ram. Allah had replaced Isma'il with a ram to be sacrificed instead.

Muslims attend the mosque on Id-ul-Adha where they pray and reflect upon Ibrahim's obedience and Allah's mercy. It is a celebration that involves spending time with family and friends. Traditionally, an animal is sacrificed and divided into three; a third is kept by the family, a third is given to friends or neighbours, and a third is given to the needy.

Id-ul-Fitr

Id-ul-Fitr, the **'Feast of the Breaking of the Fast'**, takes place at the end of Ramadan and begins at the first sighting of the new moon in the tenth month of the Islamic calendar.

Muslims give thanks to Allah for giving them the strength to fast for a month. To celebrate, they go to the mosque to pray and listen to a sermon before returning home to share their first daytime meal in a month with family and friends. Cards and presents are usually exchanged.

Muslims also give a special zakah so that those less fortunate can join in with the celebrations. After a month of fasting, Muslims feel greater empathy towards those who go hungry. Around the UK, Muslim communities hold festivals, which are attended by many non-Muslims, creating a strong sense of community between Muslims and non-Muslims.

Ashura

Ashura takes place on the tenth day of Muharram, the first month in the Islamic calendar. It is hugely important for Shi'a Muslims, as it commemorates the day Husayn, grandson of Muhammad, was killed.

The ten days up to, and including, Ashura is a period of mourning. Shi'a Muslims wear black and take part in **passion plays** (re-enactments of the story of Husayn). Some Shi'as also harm themselves to remember Husayn's suffering, though this is banned in many countries.

Ashura was originally a compulsory day of fasting for all Muslims but when Muhammad made fasting a part of Ramadan, it became voluntary on Ashura. Sunni Muslims now see Ashura as the Day of Atonement.

daydream EDUCATION

I am a Jew

Judaism is the religion of the Jewish people. Jews are guided by the Torah.

God

I worship God. I believe he is the one true almighty God who spoke to Abraham. I believe I am one of God's chosen people.

Synagogue

The synagogue is our holy temple where we go to worship. It is the centre of our community where we go to meet other Jews, study and ask for religious advice.

Ten Commandments

I follow the Ten Commandments. These are the laws which were given to Moses by God on Mount Sinai. They teach me how to live a good life.

Shabbat

Shabbat is the seventh day of the Jewish week on which God rested after Creation. Shabbat lasts from sunset on Friday to sunset on Saturday. Every Friday, my family shares a Shabbat meal of kosher food.

Worship

Our worship is led by the rabbi who reads from the Torah. The word Torah comes from the Hebrew for 'law' or 'teaching' and its words are meant to guide us in life. It should never be touched by hand so it is always read with a yad.

Pesach

We celebrate the Feast of Passover (Pesach) to commemorate the liberation from slavery of the Children of Israel who were led out of Egypt by Moses.

Branches of Judaism

Orthodox Jews believe that the Torah and the Talmud are of divine origin and contain the exact words of God. They strictly follow the teachings of the Torah, rejecting modern interpretations.

Progressive Jews see the Torah and Talmud as the interpretation of the word of God by mankind. They believe that traditional Jewish practices can be adapted to suit modern life.
There are two types of Progressive Jews:

Reform Jews

Reform Jews follow a mix of old and new traditions. Men and women are completely equal and sit together for religious services. Both men and women can be rabbis.

Liberal Jews

Liberal Jews believe in total equality between all people. They teach that following any of the Mitzvot (Jewish laws) is the personal choice of the individual.

The Nature of God

Judaism is a monotheistic religion – it teaches that there is only one God.
'Hear, O Israel, the Lord our God, the Lord is One.' **(Deuteronomy 6:4, NIV)**

Jews believe that God has certain characteristics.

God is:		
	One	Jews believe that God is the absolute one. Unlike Christians, they do not believe that God has many different forms (the Trinity).
	The Creator	God is the creator of everything. Everything in the universe was created by God.
	The Law-Giver and Judge	God provided Jews with **mitzvot**; a set of rules or commandments that Jews should obey. Jews believe that God judges the actions of all human beings and that this will determine their fate for the afterlife.
	Loving and Merciful	God cares for his creations and only wants the best for them. He is said to be *'slow to anger, abounding in love and faithfulness'* **(Exodus 34:6, NIV)**. God is just, but always merciful: *'I will have mercy on whom I will have mercy, and I will have compassion on whom I will have compassion.'* **(Exodus 33:19, NIV)**. He will forgive the repentant.

Jews will sometimes write 'G–d' instead of 'God'. This is because some Jews do not believe in writing God's name in a place where it could be damaged or erased, so write 'G–d' out of respect.

Shekinah

Shekinah is a Hebrew word which means 'dwelling' or 'settling'. It is used to describe God's divine presence in a particular place. Shekinah helps Jews to feel close to God and feel His presence in their daily lives on earth. It is said to be felt most profoundly when people are gathered in worship.

'Whenever ten are gathered for prayer, there the Shekinah rests.' **(Talmud Sanhedrin 39a)**

A feminine word, Shekinah is believed to represent the feminine qualities of God, such as gentleness and compassion.

The Problem of Evil

God is believed to be **omnipotent** (all-powerful), **omniscient** (all-knowing), **omnipresent** (everywhere at once) and **benevolent** (loving).

These characteristics can make it difficult for some people to understand why God would allow evil and suffering in the world. This is particularly challenging when considering historical events such as the Shoah (Holocaust), where millions of Jews were killed in the worst genocide in history.

Jews deal with this problem by their belief that humans cannot always understand suffering, but must maintain their faith in God and do all they can to overcome it. They also believe that humans were given free will; evil exists in the world because people choose to carry out bad actions.

daydream
EDUCATION

The Sacred Texts

The **Tanakh** and the **Talmud** are the Jewish sacred texts. They are the most important sources of authority in Judaism.

The Tanakh

The Tanakh is the primary sacred text for Jews. It contains the same books as the Christian Old Testament, but in a different order and with some slight differences.

T A N A K H

TORAH

NEVI'IM (Prophets)

KETUVIM (Writings)

1

The Torah is the first five books of the Tanakh. Jews believe that it was given to the prophet Moses by God. Therefore, Jews see the Torah as the most important of the Jewish texts. It contains the mitzvot (including the Ten Commandments) and is treated with great respect.

2

The Nevi'im traces the history of Judaism. It is divided into two parts: The Former Prophets and the Latter Prophets.

3

The Ketuvim contains holy writings, including poetry, prophecy and history. Though the writings are believed to have been divinely inspired, they have less authority than the Nevi'im and Torah.

Remember: The word 'Torah' can be used to refer to the whole of the Tanakh, the first five books, or to all Jewish teachings.

The Talmud

The Talmud is a collection of writings that cover the history, law, culture, traditions and teachings of Judaism. It consists of two parts: the **Mishnah** and the **Gemara**.

Mishnah

This is a written record of the Oral Torah compiled by Jewish scholars. It teaches Jews how to interpret and follow the mitzvot.

Gemara

This is a written record of discussions about the Mishnah and is often taken into account when debating ethical issues.

There are two versions of the Talmud: the Jerusalem Talmud and the Babylonian Talmud. Usually, when Jews speak about the Talmud, they are referring to the more detailed Babylonian version.

The Afterlife

The afterlife in Judaism is known as **olam ha-ba**, meaning 'the world to come'. There are several different beliefs within Judaism about what olam ha-ba will be like.

Sheol	Originally, Jews believed that life after death took place in a shadowy underworld called **Sheol**, where the souls of the dead remained for eternity.
Gehinnom	The idea of Sheol later developed into **Gehinnom**. Although this is translated literally as 'hell', it is, in fact, a place of cleansing for the soul. No soul remains in Gehinnom longer than 12 months; those who are worthy will progress to Gan Eden, whereas sinners will either be punished for eternity or **annihilated** (cease to exist).
Gan Eden	Jews are taught that those who lead righteous lives and maintain the covenants will go to Gan Eden. There are no clear teachings on what to expect in **Gan Eden**, so scholars still debate whether this is a physical location, a spiritual place or a state of mind. All agree, however, that those in Gan Eden will feel the presence of God.

Judgement

Jews believe that when they die, God will judge them on their actions before deciding on their fate in the afterlife. Some Jews believe that judgement happens immediately after death. Others believe this will not happen until the Day of Judgement, when the Messiah arrives.

Resurrection

There is another belief that there will be a resurrection of the dead. However, there is debate over whether this means a physical resurrection of the body or a spiritual resurrection of the soul.

'Multitudes who sleep in the dust of the earth will awake: some to everlasting life, others to shame and everlasting contempt.' (Daniel 12:2, NIV)

Some Jews do not believe in the afterlife at all. However, all Jews are encouraged to live good earthly lives for the benefit of Earth and mankind, not just for the rewards that may come in the afterlife.

'Be not like servants who serve their master on the condition of receiving a reward.' **(Ethics of the Fathers 1:3)**

The Messiah

Messiah means 'anointed one'. It was originally used to describe the kings of Israel, as it was believed that the spirit of God resided with them. However, many Jews now use the term to describe the promised leader and saviour of their people.

Jews believe that the Messiah will:

- be a male born of human parents and in no way divine (godlike).
- be a descendant of King David.
- reunite the Jewish people, restore Jewish law and rebuild the Temple in Israel.

Before the Messiah's arrival, it is believed that there will be a time of conflict.

The Prophet Elijah will announce the coming of the Messiah, who will resurrect the dead so that God can judge them on their actions on the Day of Judgement.

The Messianic Age

It is believed that the Messiah will bring the **Messianic Age**; a time of peace and abundance where Jews will return to Israel and all will acknowledge the one true God.

There are different beliefs between Jewish groups about what the Messianic Age will be like.

Orthodox Jews

We believe that the Messiah will be a real person and that he will rule wisely and fairly over all Jews. We think there will be a literal resurrection of the body, so it is important that our bodies are not damaged after death. For this reason, cremation is forbidden; only burial is allowed.

Progressive Jews

Many Progressive Jews believe that the Messiah is symbolic. We do not think that the Messianic Age will be brought about by the actions of one person; it will involve all of us doing what is right. The soul will be resurrected, but not the body, so cremation is allowed.

37

Jewish Laws & Principles

Jews believe that they have a covenant with God which makes them God's 'chosen people'. This does not mean that they think they are better than everybody else, but that they have a duty to follow a righteous life in obedience to God.

God's Covenant with Abraham

The first covenant was between God and Abraham (the father of Judaism). Abraham was told by God to leave his home and go to the **Promised Land** of Canaan to become father of a great nation.

'Go from your country... to the land I will show you. I will make you into a great nation, and I will bless you; I will make your name great, and you will be a blessing.' **(Genesis 12:1-2, NIV)**

Despite their old age and the fact that Abraham and his wife, Sarah, had never been able to have children, God blessed them with a child – Isaac. He also promised Abraham that he would protect his family and their descendants as his chosen people. In return, Abraham and his people (the **Israelites**) were to obey God and lead righteous lives.

Like Abraham, all male descendants were to be circumcised as a symbol of the covenant.

God's Covenant with Moses

The second covenant was between God and Moses (the founder of Judaism).

After fleeing famine in Canaan, the Israelites had been forced into slavery in Egypt for 400 years. Moses was chosen by God to lead his people back to Canaan (known as the **Exodus**). God promised to keep Moses and the Israelites safe if they agreed to obey him and keep his covenant.

'Now, if you obey me fully and keep my covenant, then out of all nations you will be my treasured possession.' **(Exodus 19:5, NIV)**

When Moses and his people reached Mount Sinai, God gave him ten laws which would form the basis of the new covenant. From this point, the Israelites were known as the **Jews**.

The Ten Commandments

I-V

I   You shall have no other gods before me.

II You shall not make for yourself an image in the form of anything... You shall not bow down to them or worship them.

III You shall not misuse the name of the Lord your God.

IV Remember the Sabbath day by keeping it holy.

V   Honour your father and your mother.

VI-X

VI   You shall not murder.

VII You shall not commit adultery.

VIII You shall not steal.

IX   You shall not give false testimony against your neighbour.

X   You shall not covet your neighbour's house.

(Exodus 20:1-17, NIV)

daydream EDUCATION

The Mitzvot

There are 613 laws (**mitzvot**) or commandments from God contained in the Torah. They guide Jews on how to use their free will to live good lives and obey God's will to help bring them closer to Him.

The most widely-accepted list of mitzvot is '**Mishneh Torah**' ('The Book of Commandments'), which was written by Maimonides in the 12th century.

mitzvot aseh: 248 of the mitzvot are positive, telling Jews what they should do.

mitzvot ta'aseh: 365 of the mitzvot are negative, telling Jews what they should not do.

Ritual mitzvot are laws that refer to how people should worship and obey God. These are between God and man. **Ethical mitzvot** teach Jews how to treat other people.

Judaism teaches that it is important to follow the mitzvot in order to live a good Jewish life, but also that humans have been given **free will** to choose how they act. Having responsibility over one's own actions means that God can judge a person on the choices they make.

The Sanctity of Human Life

Sanctity of life is the idea that life is special or holy as it was given as a gift from God. This influences Jewish beliefs on many issues such as contraception, war, abortion, euthanasia and medicine.

Pikuach nefesh means 'saving a life' and follows the principle of pikuach nefesh doche Shabbat. It states that life is so important, any law can be broken in order to preserve it, including Shabbat.

Organ donation is controversial. Some Jews believe that saving a life through organ donation is a gift, whereas others believe that it interferes with the burial process of keeping the body whole.

Key Moral Principles

Jews believe in the importance of Justice, kindness, charity and repairing the world (**tikkun olam**).

'He has shown you, O mortal, what is good. And what does the Lord require of you? To act justly and to love mercy and to walk humbly with your God.' (Micah 6:8, NIV)

The Torah helps to guide Jews on how to care for others, look after the environment and punish those who break God's laws.

Tzedakah: Jews believe that it is important to support those in need. However, Tzedakah is not just about charitable contributions, but about justice and righteousness.

Tikkun olam (repairing the world): Jews believe they have a responsibility to look after the world and make it a better place as God's wondrous creation; humans have no right to damage it.

Kashrut

Kashrut is a special set of laws in the Torah which tells Jews what food they are allowed to eat. Permitted food is known as **kosher**, whereas banned or 'torn' food is called **treifah**.

Kosher — The following foods are allowed:

- Animals that chew the cud and have cloven hooves (e.g. cows and sheep)
- Sea creatures with fins and scales
- Poultry
- Animals killed by a trained person using a clean slit across the throat (to drain the blood, which is treifah). The slaughter must be witnessed by a rabbi.

Treifah — The following foods are not allowed:

- Animals that do not chew the cud like pigs, or that do not have cloven hooves like hares
- Blood
- Meat and dairy together (The Torah states: 'You shall not boil a kid in its mother's milk')
- Certain birds other than poultry (e.g. birds of prey)
- Certain foods that have not been prepared or cooked by a Jewish person

Orthodox Jews are likely to observe kashrut more strictly than some Progressive Jews.

The Synagogue, Worship & Prayer

The Synagogue

A synagogue is a Jewish place of worship. There are four common key features in every synagogue.

Aron Hakodesh (The Ark)

The **aron hakodesh, or holy ark**, is the centre of worship in the synagogue. Set on the wall of the synagogue that faces Jerusalem, the ark (usually a cabinet or alcove) is used to store the Torah. The ark is opened only during special prayers and when removing the Torah.

Sefer Torah (The Scroll of the Torah)

The **Sefer Torah** is handwritten by a **sofer** (Jewish scribe) and stored inside the ark. Covered by either a cloth or case, it should not be touched by hand. Being asked to read from the Torah is seen as a great honour. As the Torah is passed around the congregation, people will bow, kiss the mantle (but not the text itself) or touch it with their **tallit** (prayer shawl).

Bimah (The Almemar)

A **bimah** is a raised area from where the Torah is read and sermons are made. Orthodox Jews usually place this in the centre of the synagogue, whereas Reform Jews are likely to have it near the ark.

Ner Tamid (The Perpetual Light)

The **ner tamid** is the light positioned above the ark representing the **menorah** (the seven-branched candlestick which stood in front of the Temple in Jerusalem). Known as the 'perpetual light', it must never be allowed to go out.

Although synagogues usually have a plain exterior, the interior is often intricately decorated. To avoid **idolatry**, Jews will not display any images of God.

*The synagogue is important to me, not only for worship, but for the sense of community. Clubs and study groups take place there regularly. As an Orthodox Jew, I must worship in a separate section of the synagogue to the men. Progressive Jews, however, have mixed seating. The **siddur** (prayer book) sets the order of prayers during services.*

daydream EDUCATION

Public Acts of Worship

Worship is important in Judaism. It forms part of the covenant with Abraham and is a mitzvah. Collective worship is linked to the idea of Shekinah, the 'presence of God'. Although Jews can worship at home, public worship is also important as it brings Jews closer to God.

Orthodox Services	Reform Services
Services are held three times a day (shacharit in the morning, minchah in the afternoon and ma'ariv at sunset).	Only certain Reform synagogues will hold services on weekdays; most do not.
Services are often led by a rabbi, but they can also be led by any man with sufficient knowledge.	Men and woman can lead services.
Services are held in Hebrew (except the sermon).	Services are partly conducted in the local language.
During some prayers and services, ten men (minyan) must be present.	The minyan can be men or women.
A hazzan (singer) sometimes leads prayers and faces Jerusalem with the rest of the congregation.	Some Reform synagogues have a hazzan. The congregation prays facing Jerusalem, but the hazzan often faces the congregation.
Orthodox Jews pray at their own pace.	Reform Jews pray at the same pace.
There is no music to accompany singing.	Singing is sometimes accompanied by music.

Prayer

Prayer is an important mitzvah that strengthens Jews' relationship with God. Jews pray to God to give thanks, ask forgiveness, or to seek help for themselves or for others.

'Worship the Lord your God, and his blessing will be on your food and water. I will take away sickness from among you.' **(Exodus 23:25, NIV)**

Many male Jews pray three times a day, either in the synagogue or at home. Women are not expected to pray or attend services as much as men, but they should pray at least twice a day. Prayer requires complete focus and concentration (kavanah), or it does not count.

The Shema is a declaration of faith in only one God. It should be said morning and night.

The Amidah (the 'standing prayer') is a set of 19 blessings that are said at weekday services. Jews should face Jerusalem whilst reciting the Amidah. A shorter version of the Amidah is used for Shabbat and festivals, but all versions will include the first and last three blessings.

As a Jewish man, I will often strap **tefillin** *(boxes containing Torah passages) to my arm and head and wear a* **tallit** *(prayer shawl) when I pray. I also wear a* **kippah** *(skull cap) as a sign of respect to God. As a Progressive Jew, I only wear this during prayer and at the synagogue. Orthodox Jews, however, will often wear these all day.*

Shabbat

In Judaism, the Sabbath is known as Shabbat and is a day of rest. It is a commemoration of the seventh day of creation, when God rested.

'Remember the sabbath day by keeping it holy.' (Exodus 20:8, NIV)

Shabbat begins just before sunset on Friday evening and lasts until sunset on Saturday evening. During Shabbat, Jews worship, reflect on their faith and come together as a community. Observing Shabbat is one of the Ten Commandments.

 Work (which can include cleaning, cooking, or spending money) is prohibited during Shabbat.

Shabbat in the Synagogue

Synagogues hold Shabbat services on Fridays and Saturdays. Although timings, format and worship will differ from synagogue to synagogue, a general overview of Shabbat services is shown below:

Friday Evening
A special service is held to welcome Shabbat (Kabbalat Shabbat) with psalms, hymns and special prayers.

Saturday Morning
The main Shabbat service is held; there are prayers from the Siddur and readings from the Torah. The whole family attends this service.

Saturday Afternoon/Evening
There is another service with prayers from the Siddur (prayer book) and readings from the Torah. Orthodox Jews often study the Torah at the synagogue afterwards.

Orthodox Jews forbid driving during Shabbat and will instead walk to the synagogue.

Shabbat in the Home

Shabbat is a time for families to celebrate together at home. It is a day of complete rest, relaxation, and rejoicing. Household chores are often performed before Shabbat, with meals being prepared in advance so Shabbat restrictions are not violated.

To mark the start of Shabbat, two candles are lit just before sunset on the Friday (this is usually done by the woman of the house). She will then cover her eyes and bless the candles. She may also wave her hands over the candles three times.

After the lighting of the candles there is a reading from Genesis 21:3 to commemorate God's day of rest after creation. A cup of wine is blessed and shared in a ritual known as Kiddush. Afterwards, Jews will wash their hands in a specific way to prepare for the Shabbat meal.

During the Shabbat meal, Jews share two loaves of sweet, plaited bread known as challot. The challot remind Jews of the food that God gave the Israelites to sustain them for their escape from Egypt.

Parents bless their children and the family will often talk about their religion and reflect upon God. The end of Shabbat is marked by a Havdalah ceremony on Saturday evening. Havdalah blessings are recited over wine, sweet-smelling spices and a special plaited candle.

daydream EDUCATION

Jewish Rituals

In Judaism, key life stages are marked by different ceremonies and rituals.

Birth

Boys and girls undergo different birth rituals.

Boys - Brit Milah

Brit milah is the Jewish ceremony in which baby boys are circumcised. It is performed as a symbol of the Jewish faith.

'Every male among you shall be circumcised... it will be the sign of the covenant between me and you.' **(Genesis 17:10-11, NIV)**

Circumcisions are performed by a **mohel** (a trained Jewish person) on the eighth day after birth. Both the father and the mohel say a blessing beforehand. After the circumcision, the Kiddush is said, the boy is given his Hebrew name and a drop of wine is placed on his tongue. The ceremony is followed by a celebratory meal.

Girls - Simchat Bat

Jewish girls have a **naming** ceremony, introduced more recently, so that girls have an equivalent ritual to mark their birth.

Simchat bat ceremonies may vary between branches of Judaism (some, such as Orthodox Jews, may not choose to include simchat bat at all), but all will include prayers, thanks, blessings and readings.

The girl will be given her Hebrew name and the parents will explain why they have selected the chosen name.

Coming of Age

When a Jewish child comes of age (13 for boys, 12 for girls), they become a **bar mitzvah** (son of commandment) or **bat mitzvah** (daughter of commandment). From this point, they are expected to follow the mitzvot (commandments).

There are bar mitzvah and bat mitzvah ceremonies to celebrate coming of age.

Jewish children will usually begin preparations for the ceremony around a year in advance, including attending lessons at the synagogue so that they are able to read from the Torah. During the ceremony, a boy or girl may be expected to give a speech, read from the Torah, give blessings and/or lead some of the prayers. This is usually followed by a big celebration.

More traditional Orthodox Jews are more likely to have a **bat hayil** (daughter of valour) ceremony where they will read a religious passage or give a speech on a Jewish topic at a service. It is reflective of the different traditional roles of men and women (women's important roles tend to be home-based).

Marriage

Marriage is a blessing from God. As well as fulfilling the commandment of procreation: *'Be fruitful and increase in number'* **(Genesis 1:28, NIV)**, marriage is a lifetime commitment to love and companionship. It is considered a duty for all Jews.

"The Lord God said, 'It is not good for the man to be alone; I will make a helper suitable for him.'" **(Genesis 2:18, NIV)**

The Wedding Ceremony

**Jewish wedding ceremonies vary between denominations.
However, some of the key practices are outlined below.**

Before the wedding day, the bride and groom often have a period of separation (this can vary from 24 hours up to a week). They may also fast before the ceremony on the wedding day.

Signing of the Ketubah	The 'marriage contract' is signed in the presence of two witnesses.
Badeken	The groom covers the bride's face with a veil (not all ceremonies include this practice).
Chuppah	The bride and groom enter the main ceremony area: a canopy known as a Chuppah. The Chuppah represents the privacy of the home that the couple will build together.
Circling the Groom	The bride circles the groom (usually seven, sometimes three, times). This creates a wall around him and is symbolic of their new home. It can also represent protection.
Kiddushin	The rabbi recites the betrothal blessings and the couple drink from a cup of wine.
Ring Ceremony	The couple exchange rings and declare their vows to each other.
Reading the Ketubah	The ketubah is read and the groom presents it to his bride.
The Seven Blessings	The seven blessings are recited over a cup of wine to give thanks to God.
Breaking the Glass	The groom breaks a glass by stamping on it; this is wrapped in a cloth or napkin to prevent injury. Some believe this is performed to remember the destruction of the Temple in Jerusalem and that joy must always be tempered.

Mourning

In Judaism, a body should not be left unattended after death, so a vigil or guardian is appointed to stay with the body. The burial should be performed as soon as possible; usually within 24 hours.

In preparation for the burial, Tahara is performed; the body is cleaned and wrapped in a plain linen shroud and should not be damaged in any way. Jewish customs specify simplicity and a natural return to the earth and burial in accordance with the Torah.

The funeral service is usually quick, involving prayers, readings and a eulogy to the deceased.

The mourning period before the funeral is known as **Aninut**. During this time, it is important to only concentrate on funeral arrangements. Kriah (tearing of clothing or cutting of black ribbon) is usually performed by family members immediately before the funeral service.

Following the burial, there is a 7-day mourning period known as **shiva**. During this time, mourners (father or mother, sister or brother, son or daughter, and spouse) remain at home. Three prayer services are conducted daily, and other mourners will visit to comfort them.

After shiva, the next period of mourning (**sheloshim**) begins, lasting until the 30th day after the funeral. This is less intense and enables mourners to resume normal duties. However, some restrictions still apply. For example, mourners must refrain from attending social events.

On the anniversary of a death (**Yahrzeit**), mourners will light candles in memory of the deceased.

Yizkor, a special memorial prayer for the departed, is recited in the synagogue four times a year.

Festivals

There are many key holy days in the Jewish calendar. Three of the most important include Rosh Hashanah, Yom Kippur and Pesach.

Rosh Hashanah

Rosh Hashanah is the Jewish New Year ('head of the year'). It is a two-day festival that marks God's creation of Adam and Eve. It begins on the first day of Tishrei, the seventh month of the Hebrew calendar, which falls in September or October.

> 'On the first day of the seventh month you are to have a day of sabbath rest, a sacred assembly commemorated with trumpet blasts. Do no regular work, but present a food offering to the Lord.' (Leviticus 23:24-25, NIV)

During Rosh Hashanah, a shofar (ram's horn) is sounded to announce the awakening of the soul and call for repentance. If Rosh Hashanah falls on Shabbat, the shofar is not blown.

On Rosh Hashanah, God inscribes the names of the righteous in the 'Book of Life' and condemns the wicked to death; those between have until Yom Kippur to perform 'teshuvah', or repentance. The ten days from the beginning of Rosh Hashanah to the end of Yom Kippur are known as **Yamim Noraim** (the 'Days of Awe').

Jews refrain from work during Rosh Hashanah and most of the day is spent in the synagogue where they pray and reflect on the past and contemplate the future.

It is traditional to eat bread and apples dipped in honey (for a 'sweet' year ahead) on Rosh Hashanah. There is also a tashlich (casting away) ceremony, where Jews will symbolically cast their sins into a body of water (e.g. a river or pond).

Yom Kippur

Yom Kippur means 'Day of Atonement' and is the most important day in the Jewish calendar. It is a chance for Jews to seek God's forgiveness for past sins.

> 'The tenth day of this seventh month is the Day of Atonement. Hold a sacred assembly and deny yourselves, and present a food offering to the Lord. Do not do any work on that day, because it is the Day of Atonement, when atonement is made for you before the Lord your God.' (Leviticus 23:27-28, NIV)

Yom Kippur is a time of fasting; most adult Jews will not eat or drink (even water) for 25 hours. During this time, they do not wear leather shoes, have sex, wear make-up or wash. This helps Jews focus on the spiritual rather than the physical.

On the evening before Yom Kippur, Jews recite a special prayer called Kol Nidre to annul any vows with God for the coming year. They spend the next day in the synagogue, reading from the Torah and praying.

Neilah is the special ceremony at the end of Yom Kippur. It is the last chance for Jews to repent and have their names written in the Book of Life before it is sealed and the gates of heaven are shut.

Sukkot is a festival of rejoicing that takes place five days after Yom Kippur. It celebrates the gathering of the harvest and commemorates the protection God provided for the children of Israel during the Exodus.

Pesach

Pesach, or Passover, commemorates the Exodus (God freeing the Israelites from slavery in Egypt).

After years of slavery, God instructed the Egyptian pharaohs to release their Israelite slaves, but they refused so he set ten devastating plagues upon them:

> '...Let my people go, so that they may worship me, or this time I will send the full force of my plagues against you and against your officials and your people...'
> (Exodus 9:13-14, NIV)

During the tenth plague, God sent the Angel of Death to kill the firstborn sons of the remaining Egyptians. The Israelites were instructed to mark their doors with lambs' blood so that the Angel of Death would 'pass over' their houses.

Pesach lasts seven or eight days. On the first (or the first two) days, there is a special meal and ritual service known as the Seder. Using a special book called the Haggadah, the story of the Exodus is retold and passed on to the next generation.

Each of the foods in the Seder meal represents a different part of the Exodus story.

Matzah	Matzah is unleavened bread made from special flour and water, but with no yeast. During the Exodus, the Israelites did not have time to wait for bread to rise so they had to eat unleavened bread.
Karpas	Karpas is a vegetable dipped in salt. The vegetable represents nature's rebirth, and the salt water represents the sadness of the ancient Jewish slaves.
Maror	Maror are bitter herbs used to symbolise the bitterness of slavery.
Charoset	Charoset is a coarse mix of nuts and apples, symbolising the mortar used by the Israelites to make bricks in Egypt.
Z'roah	Z'roah is a lamb bone, which is not eaten. It symbolises the Pesach lamb sacrifice that each family offered on Passover eve in the Temple in Jerusalem.
Baytsah	Baytsah is a hard-boiled and roasted egg, which is not eaten. It represents fertility and the cycle of life. It also symbolises the festival sacrifice made in the Temple in Jerusalem.

There are also four cups of wine placed on the table to symbolise the four promises made by God in Exodus 6:6-7. A cup is sometimes also left for Prophet Elijah, whom the Jews believe will arrive to announce the beginning of the Messianic Age.

daydream EDUCATION

Family Life

Christians, Jews and Muslims all believe that family is key for ensuring that children are brought up in a loving, protected and stable environment where they can learn about their faith.

✝ Christianity

For Christians, the purpose of family is to fulfil God's command to procreate and to provide a stable environment for children to be brought up in their faith. Parents have a duty to *'bring [their children] up in the training and instruction of the Lord'* (**Ephesians 6:4, NIV**). They can do this by attending church, sending children to Sunday School and celebrating festivals together.

✡ Judaism

Raising a family is an important Jewish duty, as it is a way for parents to pass on their faith. Jewish parents have a duty to educate their children on Judaism, and the home is where they are first exposed to Jewish practices and traditions, including Shabbat. As well as home worship, children attend synagogues, or 'shul', where they study the Torah and Talmud.

☾★ Islam

The family is vitally important in Islam. Muslims believe it provides stability within society and strengthens the **ummah** (Muslim community) as a whole. Muslim parents have a duty to educate their children in their faith by sending them to **madrasah** (Islamic school) and teaching them to fast and pray. The first words a child hears when it is born are 'Allah is great.'

In all three religions, children are taught to honour and look after their parents.

Types of Families

Most religions regard the nuclear family, with a mother and father, as the most beneficial for children, as it provides them with both male and female role models. However, as attitudes to marriage, same-sex relationships and divorce have become more accepting, other family structures have become more prominent in society.

Single-parent family	Reconstituted family	Extended family	Same-sex parent family
One parent brings up a child without a partner.	Divorced parents remarry to form a stepfamily.	Children, parents and other family members live together as one.	Two partners of the same sex bring up a child.

Christianity

Christians traditionally teach that marriage should be a commitment between a man and a woman. As such, they may feel that the idea of same-sex and single-parent families contradict this teaching. However, some Christians believe that they should 'love the sinner but hate the sin'. Though not ideal, they believe these families should still be made welcome in the church.

Judaism

Jews emphasise the importance of the traditional family, as this supports the Jewish duty to procreate and raise children in their faith. However, Jews are generally supportive of all families, with many progressive and conservative Jews being more accepting of single-parent, same-sex and reconstituted families.

Islam

Islam teaches the importance of blood relatives and the extended family. Despite many traditional Muslims rejecting the idea of same-sex families, conservative Muslims are more supportive of alternative family setups. Mothers are particularly respected in Islam: *'And We have enjoined upon man, to his parents, good treatment. His mother carried him with hardship and gave birth to him with hardship...'* (**Surah 46:15**).

Sex & Relationships

Sex
The physical and intimate way of showing affection within a personal relationship, which can lead to procreation

Cohabitation
To live with somebody without being married to them; a way some couples use to assess their compatibility before marriage

Extramarital Sex
To have sex with someone who is not your husband or wife whilst still being married; also known as adultery

Contraception
Any temporary or permanent measure that prevents a woman from becoming pregnant

Chastity
To remain sexually pure, or a virgin, until marriage

Homosexuality
To be sexually attracted to someone of the same gender

Celibacy
To have no sex, usually as part of a religious vow

Procreation
To produce offspring i.e. to have children

Promiscuity
To have casual sex with multiple partners

Premarital Sex
To have sex with someone before marriage

Purpose of Sex

Procreation is important for the continuation of human life. Many religious people believe that sex is a gift from God and is to be enjoyed because it brings the couple closer together. It is natural and should be part of married life.

Jews, Muslims and many Christians believe that couples have a duty to have sex for pleasure and not just for procreation.

However, Catholicism supports the idea that the sole purpose of sex is to have children – *'Be fruitful and increase in number'* (Genesis 1:28, NIV). Because of this, the religion opposes artificial contraception.

Cohabitation

More couples are choosing to cohabit before getting married. However, cohabitation is discouraged by most religions.

Some couples will cohabit before they fully commit to marriage. This helps ensure that they get along with each other in a day-to-day living situation and are compatible enough for marriage.

daydream
EDUCATION

Premarital Sex

Many religions, including Christianity, Judaism and Islam, teach that premarital sex is wrong and that couples should wait until they are married before having sex. Chastity is seen as an expression of dignity and respect for yourself and your future spouse.

Promiscuity is viewed as wrong because sex is an expression of love. Having many sexual partners devalues sex, makes people feel vulnerable and can cause STIs. Muslims are not allowed to mix freely with the opposite sex after reaching puberty to avoid sexual relations taking place.

Polygamy

Most religions forbid polygamy (more than one husband or wife). Religious law in Islam allows men up to four wives, but each wife must agree to this. All wives must be treated the same. However, British Muslims can only have one wife out of respect for British law and culture.

Homosexuality

Despite most people in the UK accepting homosexuality, many religions forbid homosexual sex. They believe that one of the main purposes of sex is procreation. Homosexual couples cannot naturally have children together.

'Do you approach males among the worlds and leave what your Lord has created for you as mates? But you are a people transgressing.' (Surah 26:165-166)

'Do not have sexual relations with a man as one does with a woman; that is detestable.' (Leviticus 18:22, NIV)

Sexual orientation is not forbidden in some religions, such as Judaism and Christianity. However, some believe that sexual urges towards someone of the same gender must never be acted upon.

Adultery / Extramarital Sex

Christians, Jews and Muslims all view extramarital sex as a grievous sin. For Christians and Jews, adultery is forbidden in the Ten Commandments:

'You shall not commit adultery.'
(Exodus 20:14, NIV)

Punishments in Islam can be far more severe; one of the purposes of Islamic marriage is lifelong commitment, and this includes remaining faithful to one another. Adultery is seen as evil:

'But whoever seeks beyond [marriage], then those are the transgressors.'
(Surah 23:7)

Contraception

Contraception is any temporary or permanent measure that prevents a woman from becoming pregnant. There are natural and artificial forms of contraception:

Natural forms of contraception	• Abstinence (having no sex at all) • Refraining from sex during ovulation (the 'rhythm' method) • Withdrawal method

Artificial forms of contraception	• Condoms form an artificial barrier to prevent the egg and sperm meeting. Condoms also reduce the risk of sexually-transmitted infections (STIs). • Hormonal pills and injections interfere with the hormone levels in women to temporarily reduce fertility. • Sterilisation operations, such as vasectomies, prevent fertility. These are more permanent measures.

Religious Teachings

Most religions accept some form of contraception for family planning or if pregnancy is likely to be harmful to the mother or child.

Christianity

The various Christian denominations have different views on contraception. Catholics are opposed to artificial contraception, as they believe it conflicts with God's intention for people to have children. However, they do sometimes accept natural methods that do not interfere unnaturally with the conception process (for example, abstaining from sex during ovulation).

Other Christian denominations are more accepting of the use of contraception within marriage as a responsible way of planning a family.

Judaism

The first command that God gave to humans was to 'be fruitful and increase in number'; in other words, Jews are expected to have children. However, views on contraception vary between different branches of Judaism.

Orthodox Jews prefer to avoid artificial contraception unless used for medical reasons (e.g. if pregnancy would pose a potential health risk to mother or child). This is because it is forbidden to waste sperm (or 'seed'). The contraceptive pill is sometimes considered an acceptable alternative.

Reform Jews are more likely to leave choices about contraception down to the individual.

Islam

Some Muslims believe contraception may be used within marriage, but only if both husband and wife consent to it. Some Muslims believe that the Prophet Muhammad said that all couples should have as many children as they can look after.

Some more conservative Muslims are against the use of contraceptives altogether, and argue that Islam regards children as a gift from God.

daydream EDUCATION

Marriage

Marriage is the legal or formal union of two people as partners in a relationship. This applied to the union of a man and a woman before same-sex marriage became legal in England, Wales and Scotland in 2014.

The Nature and Purpose of Marriage

Some people argue that marriage is key for stability and financial security and forms the basis for family life. Many religious people get married for these reasons as well as their own religious teachings.

Christianity
Christians believe that marriage is a sacred gift from God and represents the union of Jesus and his Church. For Christians, the purpose of marriage is to provide lifetime love and companionship and a stable environment in which to raise children.

Judaism
Marriage is an important part of Jewish family life. Jews believe that marriage is an ideal state; a union of two people to complete each other and 'become one flesh' (Genesis 2:24, NIV). Having children is also a key purpose for marriage.

Islam
Marriage is an exchange of contracts and is seen as a lifelong commitment between two people. Love is expected to develop but it is not the main purpose of marriage; the expectation to have children and continue the religious tradition is most important.

Same-Sex Marriage

The legalisation of same-sex marriage in 2014 shows how attitudes have shifted over time. The British Social Attitudes survey revealed that in 1983, only 17% of people surveyed agreed with same-sex relationships. This had rocketed to 64% in 2016.

Christians, Jews and Muslims have different views on same-sex marriage.

Christianity
Christians, especially Catholic Christians, traditionally teach that marriage should be between a man and a woman. However, many Christians believe that they should show love to all and support those who want to marry, regardless of gender.

Judaism
Some Jews, including many orthodox Jews, believe that same-sex marriage goes against the teachings of the Torah. However, several denominations of Judaism are more supportive of homosexuality, allowing same-sex marriages in their synagogues.

Islam
Islam expects men and women to marry so they can have children; this is a duty in Islam, so many Muslims are against same-sex marriage. However, many Muslims tolerate same-sex marriage and homosexuality, although they do not encourage it.

Divorce

The legal ending of a marriage.

Divorce and UK Law

To get a legal divorce in the UK, you must have been married for a minimum of one year; your marriage must be legally recognised by UK law; you must have a permanent home in the UK; and you must have a valid reason recognised by the court and evidence to show that the marriage has broken down irretrievably. According to UK law, there are five recognised grounds for divorce: adultery; unreasonable behaviour; desertion; living apart for two years and both agreeing to the divorce; and living apart for five years where no consent is needed.

D — Divorce

All religions frown upon divorce but do accept that sometimes it is necessary (Catholicism, however, does not recognise divorce). Divorce must be the last resort.

I — Interventions

Family, friends and the religious community will intervene and help the couple to reconcile. Marriage joins families together, not just a couple, so everyone will do what they can to help save the marriage.

V — Vows

Spouses have promised each other that they will remain married for life no matter how difficult the marriage becomes. They are expected to treat each other with dignity and respect, and to remember the promises they have made. Some people regard the vows as being sacred because they were made in front of God.

O — Order of Service

During the wedding ceremony, the couple are asked if they understand the contract they are entering into and if they want to marry. From this moment on, the couple have a duty to each other to try to make the marriage work.

R — Remarriage

Most religions teach that, after divorce, each person is free to remarry and is encouraged to do so. However, Catholicism does not recognise divorce and believes that those who remarry after a civil divorce are committing adultery. Such individuals will be prohibited from taking Holy Communion and attending Mass.

C — Children

Divorce can be very damaging and can hurt many people, not just the couple. Children must be protected at all times. The couple should try to work out their differences to ensure that their children have a stable home life and upbringing.

E — Education

'The most detestable act that Allah has permitted is divorce.' (Islam)
'What God has joined together, let no one separate.' (Christianity)

daydream
EDUCATION

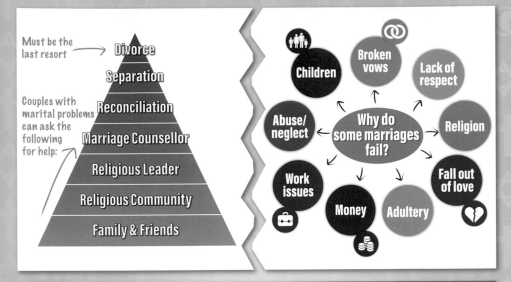

Must be the last resort →

Divorce
Separation
Reconciliation

Couples with marital problems can ask the following for help: ↗

Marriage Counsellor
Religious Leader
Religious Community
Family & Friends

Children
Broken vows
Lack of respect
Abuse/neglect
Why do some marriages fail?
Religion
Work issues
Money
Adultery
Fall out of love

Religious Teachings About Divorce

Christianity

Divorce is seen as a negative thing as it marks the end of both a loving relationship and a promise made to love each other forever. Many Christians allow divorce in difficult circumstances; for example, if a partner is treated badly, abused or is made to be deeply unhappy. They must then apply the principle of the most loving thing to do, which in some cases, is to divorce. Some Anglicans (Church of England) will allow a divorcee to remarry in a church. Protestants, on the other hand, do allow remarriage but this cannot take place in a church.

Catholic Christianity

Divorce is not acceptable in Catholicism and is considered a sin. However, the church does grant annulments which cancel the existence of the marriage. The marriage becomes void and you are free to marry another person in the church.
An annulment can only be granted if the marriage is found to be invalid (i.e. not meeting the requirements of a sacramental marriage).

Judaism

Some Jews do not accept a civil divorce as the legal ending of their marriage. They must follow the religious procedures for divorce. The husband must give his wife a document of divorce (a **gett**) and receive approval from a rabbinical court (beit din).
'If a man marries a woman who becomes displeasing to him because he finds something indecent about her...he writes her a certificate of divorce, gives it to her and sends her from his house...' **(Deuteronomy 24:1, NIV)**

Islam

In Islam, divorce is seen as the last resort. Although divorce is allowed, it is discouraged, and every effort should be made to reconcile.

A man may divorce his wife by announcing his intention to divorce three times over a three-month period. A woman may also instigate divorce if her husband is deemed unfit to carry out his marital duties.

Gender Discrimination

Most religions teach that all men and women are equal and should be treated equally. However, religions also view men and women as different, with separate roles to play. Each role is of equal importance.

 Traditionally, women's roles involved looking after the family and running the household. Women were also supposed to obey their husbands.

 Although the rules of religions state that women must be treated equally, this has not always been the case within religions and society.

 Traditionally, the role of men was to go to work and provide for the family financially.

Women have had to fight hard for equal rights. Beginning with the creation of the suffragette movement, significant changes regarding women's rights occurred throughout the 20th century in the UK.

1918
Women aged 30+ allowed to vote

1961
Married women allowed contraceptive pill

1979
Britain's first female Prime Minister, Margaret Thatcher, took office

1919
Sex Disqualification (Removal) Act passed allowing women to work in any profession

1973
Female stockbrokers first admitted to London Stock Exchange

1994
Church of England appoints first female vicar

1865
First female doctor, Elizabeth Garrett Anderson, licensed

1967
Abortion Act passed

1903
Suffragette movement formed

1928
Women aged 21+ allowed to vote (same as men)

1970
Equal Pay Act passed

2014
Church of England appoints first female bishop

1915
First female police constable, Edith Smith, appointed

1964
Women become legal owners of the money they earn, and are able to inherit property

1975
Sex Discrimination Act makes it illegal to discriminate against women in employment, education and training

daydream
EDUCATION

Is there gender discrimination in religion?

Yes

Saudi Arabia is a Muslim country which banned women from driving until 2017.

Some religions require women to wear traditional clothing.

Some traditional men still see women as inferior.

Jewish women traditionally lead Shabbat rituals at home.

Some religions expect women to stay at home.

In some places of worship women and men are separated.

Some women are forbidden to lead prayers in places of worship.

Some religions allow men, but not women, to have polygamous relationships.

No

Women are free to work as long as they follow religious rules.

Most religious believers support the UN Charter.

Many religions encourage women to get an education.

Some religions believe that people will be judged on how they treat others.

In many countries, Muslim women may choose whether to wear a headscarf.

In some Christian denominations and Reform Judaism, women may lead worship.

Some holy books suggest that men are superior to women – for example:

'I do not permit a woman to teach or to assume authority over a man; she must be quiet. For Adam was formed first, then Eve…it was the woman who was deceived and became a sinner. But women will be saved through childbearing…'
(1 Timothy 2:12-15, NIV)

'Men are in charge of women by [right of] what God has given one over the other and what they spend [for maintenance] from their wealth.'
(Surah 4:34)

However, many religions have moved away from these teachings and look to leaders such as Jesus and Muhammad, who taught about love, compassion, fairness and equality.

Origins of the Universe & Life

No one knows exactly how the universe began. Most religions believe that the universe and everything within it was designed and created by God. The two main scientific theories are the **Big Bang Theory** and the **Theory of Evolution**.

The Big Bang Theory

The Big Bang Theory is the prevailing cosmological explanation for the origins of the universe. In 1927, Catholic priest and physicist Georges Lemaître concluded that there must have been a point of singularity from which the universe started and that all matter in the universe was concentrated in a single point. It is estimated that approximately 13.7 billion years ago, a huge explosion caused the rapid expansion of matter and the creation of the universe and everything within it. The universe is still expanding today, which is important evidence for this theory.

The Theory of Evolution

In 1859, Charles Darwin published *On the Origin of Species*, in which he claimed that all life on earth originated from a common ancestor. Darwin stated that all life has evolved from simple cells over millions of years through common descent (reproduction) and natural selection, where species that are better adapted to their environment survive. Scientists have found much evidence to support his theory through genetics and DNA comparisons. Evolution continues to happen today.

Religious Teachings

Christians, Jews and Muslims share very similar views on creation, believing that God created the world and everything in it.

Traditional literalists or creationists take the holy accounts of creation literally and believe that the world was created by God in seven days. They do not necessarily oppose the theory of evolution, but they do not believe that humans evolved from apes. They believe that God created humans with a soul, giving them a special purpose and bond with God. In contrast, many people believe that the story of creation is a symbolic description, rather than a literal one, that shows the power of God as Creator.

The Christian and Jewish holy accounts of creation are both found in Genesis. This states that God created the world in six days and rested on the seventh. The Qur'an also offers a similar account of creation for Muslims, stating that Allah created the heavens and the earth and all that lies between them in six days.

> *'In the beginning God created the heavens and the earth.'*
> **(Genesis 1:1, NIV)**

> *'Then God blessed the seventh day and made it holy, because on it he rested from all the work of creating that he had done.'*
> **(Genesis 2:3, NIV)**

> *'Have those who disbelieve not considered that the heavens and the earth were a joined entity, and we separated them and made from water every living thing? Then what will they not believe?'*
> **(Surah 21:30)**

> *'It is God who created the heavens and the earth and whatever is between them in six days.'*
> **(Surah 32:4)**

daydream
EDUCATION

Similarities Between Scientists and Creationists

Creationists believe that the world was made in a set order over seven days, whereas evolutionists believe that the world was formed in a set order over millions of years. The orders of creation and evolution are very similar, but the time is very different. What if 'seven days' was not a literal translation and the days of creation represented different ages? After all, the Hebrew word for *day* is the same as *age*.

Creation According to Creationists

Evolution According to Scientists

Creation According to Creationists		Evolution According to Scientists
Light and darkness	1	Explosion and planet cools
Sky and oceans	2	Water and air
Dry land and plant life	3	Dry land
Sun, moon and stars	4	Plants
Sea creatures and birds	5	Birds and fish
Animals and people	6	Animals
Rest	7	People

daydream
EDUCATION

57

Stewardship

All religions teach that the Earth is sacred or special and should be looked after. All major religions, except Buddhism, believe that the world was created by God and that it is our responsibility to look after God's creation.

Key Words

Wonder: A feeling of amazement at the beauty and complexity of the universe

Awe: A feeling of respect for the universe

Creator: The idea that God made the world and that, therefore, we should respect his creations

Stewardship: The responsibility to look after the planet, which is taught by most religions

Dominion: Ownership or ruling over the planet; the idea that the world belongs to humans

Problems

Global Warming: The burning of fossil fuels has caused an increase in the concentration of greenhouse gases in the atmosphere. This has resulted in the Earth heating up and rising sea levels due to the melting of huge ice caps.

Destruction of Habitats: Deforestation and the clearing of land for building and agriculture are having a hugely detrimental effect on the natural habitats of animals.

Pollution: Land, air, river and sea pollution are all contributing to harming the environment.

The growth in the human population is putting a strain on the global environment and natural resources.

Waste: The increasing world population is generating more and more waste, which is harmful to the environment.

Acid Rain: Atmospheric pollution can result in acid rain, which is corrosive to the environment and harmful to animals.

Use of Natural Resources: The Earth's natural resources are being consumed at an alarming rate, and will eventually run out.

Solutions

Sustainable Development

International Efforts: Many countries around the world are working together to reduce fossil fuel emissions and protect the planet.

Renewable Energy: Using renewable energy (such as solar, wind and tidal energy) instead of fossil fuels will reduce pollution, cause less damage to the environment and reduce global warming.

Recycling: Reusing waste materials saves resources and reduces landfill.

Development that meets the needs of the present without compromising the ability of future generations to meet their own needs.

Conservation: Protecting things found in nature, such as endangered animals and rainforests, helps to prevent damage to the ecosystem.

58

daydream EDUCATION

Religious Teachings

Christianity

Originally, Christians believed that dominion over the Earth meant that they could use the world however they pleased. Now, they understand that the world has limited resources and that their power over the Earth includes a responsibility to look after it. They believe that God created the world and appointed humans as stewards of His planet.

Judaism

Jews believe they have a responsibility to look after the world as God's wondrous creation and that humans have no right to damage it. They also believe they have a responsibility to make the world a better place. This is known as **tikkun olam** (repairing the world): the idea of building a world for eternity.

Islam

Muslims believe that the world belongs to Allah and that humans are its stewards, or '**khalifah**'. Muslims must look after the world for Allah and for future generations and will be punished or rewarded at the Day of Judgement depending on how well they carry out this task.

The Use of Animals for Food

Christianity, Judaism and Islam all believe that animals should be treated well. Some people think it is wrong to use animals for food; as God's creatures, they should not be harmed. For this reason, some choose vegetarian or vegan lifestyles. Other people might argue that humans were designed to include meat in their diets, but that any animals used for food should be treated humanely.

Judaism has special laws about meat, which are outlined in the Torah. The only types of meat that may be eaten are cattle and game that have 'cloven hooves' and 'chew the cud'. Meat that can be eaten must come from animals that have been slaughtered humanely through '**koshering**', ensuring that all blood is removed.

'*And wherever you live, you must not eat the blood of any bird or animal.*' (Leviticus 7:26, NIV)

Islam also has special laws about food. Only **halal** (permissible) foods that adhere to Islamic law can be consumed by Muslims. All pork and foods containing blood are forbidden, and animals must be slaughtered in a swift and merciful manner, so they do not suffer in any way.

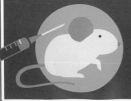

Animal Experimentation

Animal experimentation is a controversial issue; many people are opposed to this because of the mistreatment and suffering of animals which may occur. However, there are others who allow it for medical and scientific reasons because it is for the greater good of mankind to find cures for diseases.

Abortion

Abortion is the deliberate premature ending of a pregnancy resulting in the death of the foetus. There are very strong opposing views on abortion and whether it should be allowed.

Sanctity of Life

Life is precious and sacred – it is a gift from God.

Most religions believe in the sanctity of life. No one has the right to take life or deny it. All life has a purpose and should be treated with respect.

Hippocratic Oath

All people who join the medical profession must sign the Hippocratic Oath in which they promise to 'do no harm'.

Some people think abortion conflicts with this oath.

Sanctity of Life

Abortion became legal in England, Scotland and Wales with the Abortion Act 1967 (it is still illegal in Northern Ireland). The Human Fertilisation and Embryology Act 1990 introduced a new upper time limit of 24 weeks.

Abortions must be performed in a registered clinic or hospital and must be agreed by two doctors. During 0–24 weeks, an abortion is permitted if:

- There is a physical or mental risk to the mother's health
- Any existing children would suffer or be at risk
- The child would be severely disabled

Many people think the limit of 24 weeks should be reduced as several premature babies born before 24 weeks have survived.

When Does Life Begin?

Conception	First heartbeat	When organs are formed	Ensoulment	When able to live outside the womb	At birth
When egg and sperm meet (Christianity)	3 weeks	12 weeks	120 days after conception (Islam)	Usually after 22 weeks	40 weeks (Judaism)

daydream EDUCATION

Pro-Life

- All life is special and has purpose and value.
- Life begins at conception.
- Every embryo has the potential to be a human and should have the right to life.
- Abortion could cause health risks during future pregnancies.
- The woman may regret the abortion, and it may weigh heavily on her conscience.
- Other relatives, for example the father, should have a say.
- There are alternatives, such as adoption. Many couples are infertile and would like to adopt.
- Children with disabilities also have the right to life.
- Abortion is irreversible.

Pro-Choice

- The actual life of the woman is more important than the potential life of the unborn child.
- Other children in the family should not suffer due to another child being born.
- If a woman is raped, she should not have to have the child.
- Desperate women may resort to dangerous alternatives.
- It is kinder to allow an abortion if the child will be severely disabled and have no quality of life.
- The child, when born, may remain unwanted and end up neglected and put into care.
- It should be the woman's choice because it is her body.

Religious Teachings

Many religions discourage abortion. Religions view life as a sacred gift from God, so only God has the right to take life. Humans are not to interfere with God's plan. There is purpose to all life and to all suffering and pain.

'You shall not murder.'
(Exodus 20:13, NIV)

'And do not kill your children for fear of poverty. We provide for them and for you. Indeed, their killing is ever a great sin.'
(Surah 17:31)

'There is no god besides me. I put to death and I bring to life.'
(Deuteronomy 32:39, NIV)

Despite the general opposition to abortion, some religious people agree that it is sometimes necessary, especially if there is a risk to the woman's physical or mental health. It is still always regrettable, and abortions should be carried out as soon as possible.

Euthanasia

Euthanasia involves deliberately killing someone painlessly to relieve suffering, especially from incurable illness. It is often referred to as mercy killing. In the UK, euthanasia is currently illegal.

Types of Euthanasia

Voluntary
Ending a person's life deliberately and painlessly at his or her request.

Active
Actively doing something to end a person's life – for example, a doctor administering a lethal injection.

Assisted Suicide
Providing a seriously ill person with the means to commit suicide.

Non-Voluntary
Ending a person's life painlessly when he or she is unable to ask, but there is good reason to believe he or she would want you to.

Passive
Withholding or withdrawing treatment, such as when medical treatment or life support is withdrawn, or a person is not resuscitated.

Arguments for 👍

It allows a more dignified death.

It allows a patient to die without pain.

Medical staff can dedicate their time to patients who have a chance of recovery.

It can relieve the burden on the family.

It may reduce medical costs.

It is kinder for the patient because it does not prolong suffering.

Arguments against 👎

New medicines could become available to cure previously incurable illnesses.

Doctors have signed the Hippocratic Oath. It is unfair to ask them to euthanise patients.

No one has the right to make a judgement on the value of another person's life.

Euthanasia is a big concern for many religious believers.

Some people feel pressurised into choosing euthanasia.

The hospice movement provides alternative palliative care and ensures patients have a good quality of life before they die.

daydream
EDUCATION

Religious Teachings

Many religions oppose euthanasia because they believe all life is sacred and should be treated with respect. Only God should decide when and how a person dies. Humans are not to interfere with God's plan. There is purpose to all life and to all suffering and pain.

Christianity

'You shall not murder.'
(Exodus 20:13, NIV)

Life is a sacred gift from God and should not be interfered with. However, some Christians believe that the Bible teaches compassion and respect. Therefore, someone should not be forced to suffer unnecessarily.

Deliberately ending a life could interfere with the natural course of a soul's departure when it leaves the body to join God.

The Catholic Church is strongly opposed to euthanasia and believes that it is a crime against life.

Judaism

'There is no god besides me. I put to death and I bring to life.'
(Deuteronomy 32:39, NIV)

Only God has the right to give life and take it away, even when it has become a burden rather than a blessing.

Although Judaism is opposed to voluntary euthanasia and suicide, some Jews believe that passive euthanasia is permissible if they think further treatment will prevent the natural departure of the soul or cause suffering. Relief of pain and suffering is a key theme in Jewish teachings.

Islam

'And it is not [possible] for one to die except by permission of God at a decree determined.'
(Surah 3:145)

All human life is given by Allah, and Allah decides how long each person will live. Life is a test, and all those suffering should turn to Allah, whom they trust will help them understand the reasons why on the Day of Judgement.

However, in circumstances where death is inevitable, the patient should be allowed to die without unnecessary procedures.

Care for the Dying

Although religious believers are generally opposed to euthanasia, they are also strongly against allowing people to suffer. They therefore try to help in the following ways:

 Helping to relieve pain through medicine

 Caring for the terminally ill in hospices

 Offering emotional and practical support to the families of those dying

 Providing spiritual and emotional care to those suffering

HOSPITAL

EMERGENCY

Life After Death

Most religions believe in the afterlife and the concept of a soul – the non-physical spiritual part of a human being. Many non-religious people also believe in the afterlife and the existence of the soul. However, some people believe that there is no such thing as a soul and that once you die, you cease to exist.

Christianity

The resurrection of Jesus gives Christians hope for eternal life.

"Jesus said to her, 'I am the resurrection and the life. The one who believes in me will live, even though they die; and whoever lives by believing in me will never die. Do you believe this?'"
(John 11:25-26, NIV)

After death, the soul remains in a state of waiting until **Judgement Day**.

If God believes you have lived a good life and that you have believed in Him, you will spend eternity in heaven with God. Non-believers and people who have led bad lives will be sent to **hell**.

An unredeemable soul will be **annihilated**.

Heaven and hell can be a physical place or a state of mind.

Roman Catholics believe in Purgatory – a place where the soul is cleansed before it enters heaven.

Death is a difficult concept to come to terms with so the belief in heaven and the afterlife is comforting to Christians.

Judaism

Jews believe in the resurrection of the dead and that there will be an era of perfect peace and prosperity called the Messianic Age.

The righteous (both Jews and non-Jews) will be resurrected to live together in the **Messianic Age**. Those who have led a sinful life will not be resurrected.

'Multitudes who sleep in the dust of the earth will awake: some to everlasting life, others to shame and everlasting contempt.'
(Daniel 12:2, NIV)

Orthodox Jews believe that the physical body is resurrected so cremation is forbidden.

Modern Jews believe that the soul must spend no more than 12 months in **Gehinnom**, where the soul is purified of its sins, before going to Gan Eden – a paradise for those who lived a righteous life. The perfectly righteous do not have to pass through Gehinnom, whereas the unrepentant wicked are cut off and never reach paradise. Although Jews have these beliefs about the afterlife, they believe it is more important to focus on this life and how to live it well.

Islam

Muslims believe in Akhirah (the afterlife) and the resurrection of the body and soul after death. It is one of the articles of faith.

After death, the body and soul will remain in **Barzakh** – a state of 'cold sleep' until the Day of Judgement. How Muslims live their earthly lives will determine how they are judged on Judgement Day. It is a Muslim's duty to be obedient to Allah.

'Indeed, those who disbelieve – never will their wealth or their children avail them against God at all, and those are the companions of the Fire; they will abide therein eternally.' **(Surah 3:116)**

On Judgement Day, Allah judges you on how you have lived your life. All will be judged, but only Muslims will go to paradise unless Allah is feeling merciful.

Those who have followed the will of Allah will be rewarded with entry into **Jannah** (paradise). Those who have lived a life of sin will go to **Jahannam** (hell).

Non-Religious Reasons for Believing in an Afterlife

Near-Death Experiences

Some people who have been close to death have reported unusual sensations such as out-of-body experiences, feelings of levitation or total serenity, and seeing bright lights.

Paranormal Activities

Unexplained phenomena, such as ghosts and mediums who claim to be able to contact the dead, are sometimes used as evidence of life after death.

Past Lives

Some people claim to have memories of previous lives, and this is sometimes used as evidence of the afterlife.

Reasons to Believe

- It provides a purpose to life.
- It is an integral part of religion.
- It encourages people to live a good life.
- It encourages morality and discipline.
- It brings comfort to the bereaved.
- It gives hope to people who have suffered.
- It teaches people to repent and to forgive.
- Some people believe there must be more after this life, as there must be some sort of reward for the unfairness and suffering on earth.

Reasons to Not Believe

- There is no evidence to support the existence of an afterlife or reincarnation.
- No one has ever returned from the dead.
- Religion and the holy books are outdated.
- People can be moral and disciplined without religion and the threat of punishment.
- Historically, teachings about heaven and hell, especially hell, were used as a means to control people.
- People who claim to have seen ghosts or remember past lives could be making these stories up.

Influence on Believers

Belief in the afterlife has a significant impact on the lives of religious believers. It teaches them about God and reminds them to obey the teachings of their faith.

It helps people cope with the idea of unfairness, cruelty and suffering in the world by reassuring them that:

- Good deeds will be rewarded
- Suffering is only temporary
- Evil people will be punished upon death

The promise of eternal life for those who believe and carry out good deeds encourages religious believers to not only follow their own routines of worship, but to look for ways to help others. This follows the idea that the reward for helping others in this life is improving your circumstances in the next life.

The punishment of the wicked also reinforces the idea of God as just. A just God makes sure people get what they deserve in the afterlife. This is one way of justifying man-made evil in the world in the eyes of many religious believers.

The Nature of God

God, the almighty Lord is **omnipotent** – all-powerful.

God is the judge. He will judge all mankind. The good will be rewarded with heaven. The bad will be punished with hell.

God is **omnipresent** – everywhere at once.

God is the guide. All must always try to think of him.

God is **transcendent** – beyond time and the material universe. He created the world but does not need to exist within it.

God is **immanent** – present and active in the world. His presence can be felt in the daily lives of those who believe.

God is **impersonal** – watching away from the world; a distant figure who rarely becomes involved in the personal lives of humans.

God is the creator of the world and everything in it.

GOD IS...

God is **omnibenevolent** – all-loving.

God has spoken and revealed himself through the prophets, teachers and holy texts.

God is one. Most of the major religions are monotheistic. They believe that there is only one god.

God is **omniscient** – all-seeing and all-knowing. Nothing happens without God's knowledge.

God is **personal** – some people believe that they can have a personal relationship with God, and that He listens to and answers their prayers.

God is **eternal** – everlasting, having no beginning and no end.

God is beyond human imagination.

daydream EDUCATION

Christianity

Christians believe in the trinity – the idea that God exists in three forms.

The Father –

God is the creator of the universe. He sustains everything. Nothing can exist without God's power.

The Son –

Jesus came to earth as God in human form to save people. His crucifixion is believed to have redeemed the sins of the world.

The Holy Spirit –

After the ascension of Jesus, God gave humans the gift of the Holy Spirit. The Spirit is God's love and power in the world that helps people today.

Judaism

Although opinions and beliefs differ within Judaism, key beliefs are shared across all denominations of the religion.

- God is one: *'Hear, Israel:*
The Lord is our God,
The Lord is one.'
(Deuteronomy 6:4, NIV)

Jews do not believe that Jesus was the son of God.

Jews are forbidden to represent God in a physical form. **God is eternal and omnipresent** and has no physical body.

Islam

Muslims believe in one god, Allah, who is all-powerful. Muhammad is the messenger of Allah.

Shahadah is the basic statement of the Islamic faith. **'There is no god but Allah** and Muhammad is the prophet of **Allah.' Tawhid** is the concept of the oneness of Allah.

Allah has 99 names in the Qu'ran, each of which describes an attribute of Allah: the Almighty, the Merciful, the Just, the Creator and the Provider.

Does God Exist?

Agnostic – A person who believes it is impossible to prove one way or another whether God exists.

Theist – A person who believes in God.

Atheist – A person who does not believe in God.

Philosophical Arguments

Design/Teleological Argument

William Paley

'The world is so perfect there must be a designer and maker.'

Just as the function of a watch requires a watchmaker, the world and everything in it must have a creator. Like a watch, the world is so perfectly designed and formed that it could not be the result of chance or accident. The only being powerful enough to create such perfection is God.

Sir Isaac Newton also added to this argument by stating that the human thumb was so complex and perfectly suited to purpose that it alone would be enough to convince him that God existed.

The fact that the world is so perfectly designed to sustain human life is further proof to many religious believers that God exists.

Cosmological Argument

Thomas Aquinas

"God does exist. God is the 'uncaused cause'."

The Cosmological, or First Cause, argument is based on logical proof that God exists and argues that nothing can create itself. The ability to defy logic and do the impossible makes God an 'uncaused cause'; in other words, an impossible thing. Only a being of such ultimate power could do the impossible.

However, some people argue that this logic is flawed as it contradicts itself: if it argues that everything must have a cause, then how could it argue that in the beginning, there was an event without a cause (The First Cause)?

For some religious believers, the cosmological argument does not conflict with the Big Bang Theory as they argue that God is the thing that caused the Big Bang in the first place.

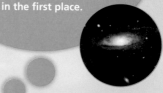

Strengths

- Knowing God exists gives meaning and purpose to life.
- Belief in God and an afterlife encourages moral behaviour.
- People have everything to gain by believing in God and nothing to lose.

Weaknesses

- Life can have meaning, purpose and morals without having a creator or designer or God.
- The arguments are only theories and assumptions. They are not proof that God exists.
- If there is no God or afterlife, dedicating one's life to God is a waste of time.

daydream
EDUCATION

God Does Exist ✓	VS	God Does Not Exist ✗
Jesus performed miracles, and miracles have been witnessed in places such as Lourdes. Many people continue to pray because they believe that God responds to, and answers, their prayers.	**Miracles & Prayers Answered**	As knowledge of technology and science expand, the more miracles can be explained. Why would miracles only happen to a select few people? Why are only a few prayers answered? Are not all humans special?
Many people from around the world claim to have had some sort of religious experience that brings them closer, and makes them more devoted to God.	**Religious Experience**	Religious experience is subjective. It rarely happens to more than one individual at a time, so it is not verifiable. People in the past have used their religious experience to justify their bad behaviour. For example, the Yorkshire Ripper reported that God told him to punish the young women he killed.
This life is a test, and all humans have been given free will to behave in the way they choose. Most evil and suffering result from human misconduct, not God.	**Evil & Suffering**	If God is omnipotent, omniscient and benevolent, why does He allow people to suffer? Why does He allow evil things to happen? Surely God would have more power and control!
All religions have sacred texts with similar teachings about God. Why would these exist if there were not some truth about God? God has revealed Himself through and to many people, such as prophets, Martin Luther King and Gandhi.	**Revelation**	An omnipotent God who wants humans to believe in Him would be better at securing believers. Why would God choose to reveal Himself to only a select few rather than to all humans?
Why is the universe so orderly, so reliable and so well designed? It could not be this way by accident!	**Nature & Numinous**	A benevolent deity ought to create a perfect world, not an imperfect one like the real world.
The founders of several world religions are believed to have had some paranormal powers that cannot be explained scientifically. For example, Jesus walked on water, and the Buddha gained the power to see his and others' past lives.	**Paranormal Activity**	Paranormal activity is not proof of God. Many religious people themselves are deeply suspicious of it.
Why did the disciples record the resurrection of Jesus if it did not happen? Why do many people believe they can remember a previous life?	**Afterlife**	There is no physical evidence of an afterlife – the main reason for believing in God.
Much of science is based on theory, not proven facts. Theories change. Religious beliefs tend not to change, suggesting that God has revealed Himself to those who believe.	**Science**	Religious arguments about God are inconsistent. Science offers theories with some evidence about creation and evolution, suggesting that there is no God.

Revelation

Revelation is God's way of making Himself and His divine will known to humans on earth. There are two main types of revelation: general revelation and special revelation.

General Revelation

General revelation is indirect – something which is available to every person, and in every place. God is revealed through the natural and physical world, reasoning and human conscience.

The Holy Books

The holy books are a key source of revelation. They give an indication of God's nature, intentions, and expectations for mankind. Many people believe that these scriptures contain God's direct word or that they were written by people under His influence.

Christianity

The Bible, written by various authors, is the key text which guides the lives of Christians. The Gospels reveal the life of Jesus Christ, including the miracles he performed.

Judaism

The Torah is the central Jewish text containing the law of God as presented to Moses. Written by various authors, it shows Jews how to live their lives and reveals God's nature.

Islam

For Muslims, **the Qur'an** is the literal word of God passed from the angel Jibril to Muhammad and then to mankind. It reveals Allah's nature and expectations.

Although their specific authors make them forms of special revelation, their availability to all can also classify them as forms of general revelation.

God in Nature

Christians, Jews and Muslims believe that nature can provide evidence of God's existence. For example, an awe-inspiring sunrise or a breathtaking mountain view can be evidence enough for some people to believe that only a God could create such things of beauty.

'...or speak to the earth, and it will teach you, or let the fish in the sea inform you. Which of all these does not know that the hand of the Lord has done this?'

(Job 12:8-9, NIV)

"When God created the first man He took him and showed him all the trees of the Garden of Eden and said to him 'See My works, how beautiful and praiseworthy they are...'"

(Midrash Kohelet Rabbah 7:28)

'He is God, the Creator, the Inventor, the Fashioner, to Him belong the best names. Whatever is in the heavens and earth is exalting him...'

(Surah 59:24)

Special revelation is direct – it only occurs for specific people, in specific places, at specific times. It is a highly personal experience, and could take the form of a prophecy, vision, dream or miracle.

Visions

A vision is an experience of seeing a spiritual being, such as an angel, a holy figure, or even God Himself. There have been many accounts throughout history of people personally receiving revelation from God through religious visions.

Many Christians believe that they have experienced visions, and the Bible contains many accounts of visions. Examples of Christian visions include:

- Jesus revealing himself to his followers after his resurrection: "Jesus said to her, 'I am the resurrection and the life. The one who believes in me will live, even though they die; and whoever lives by believing in me will never die. Do you believe this?'" **(John 11:25-26, NIV)**
- Bernadette Soubirous claimed to have seen the Virgin Mary at Lourdes in 1858. It remains an important pilgrimage site today after claims of its miraculously healing waters.

There are many Jewish examples of visions in the Torah. These include:

- God tested Abraham's loyalty by ordering him to sacrifice his own son. When God saw that Abraham was loyal, He revealed himself again and showed mercy by stopping the sacrifice.
- The angel of God spoke to Moses and appeared to him in the form of a burning bush, before giving Moses instructions to tell the Jews that He would help them.

The Qur'an contains accounts of visions from key Islamic figures. These include:

- The prophets of Islam were all visited by the angels, the messengers of Allah. These include **Ibrahim** (Abraham), **Dawud** (David) and **Isa** (Jesus).
- The angel Jibril revealed the first words of the Qur'an and commanded Muhammad to spread the word of Allah. Jibril appeared many more times to reveal more of the Qur'an.

Prayer is another way in which people claim to have received spiritual messages from God. Some claim that God has communicated with them in response to their prayers.

Miracles

A miracle can be defined as an amazing and extraordinary event that cannot be explained by the laws of science and nature. Many people believe that miracles are proof of God's existence.

The Bible, Torah and Qur'an all contain examples of miracles:

Christianity

Jesus carries out many miracles, showing his divine nature and relationship with God the Father.

Judaism

A key example of a miracle is the plagues of Egypt, where Jewish people were saved through God's intervention.

Islam

Muslims regard the Qur'an itself as a miracle as it is the word of Allah upon earth.

Revelations can provide evidence of God's characteristics. For example:

Omnipotent · Omnipresent · Personal · Impersonal · Immanent · Transcendent

Revelations of God's nature can be provided through written records in scripture and His presence in daily life. For example, a beautiful sunset may provide evidence of an immanent and omnipresent God; his existence is always evident in the natural world all around us.

Peacemaking & Victims of War

Promoting peace and helping victims of war is important to Christianity, Judaism and Islam. There are many religious organisations who work for peace and provide aid to war victims.

Justice, Forgiveness and Reconciliation

All three Abrahamic religions promote justice, forgiveness and reconciliation to maintain peace.

 'Father, forgive them, for they do not know what they are doing.' **(Luke 23:34, NIV)**

 'Do not seek revenge or bear a grudge against anyone among your people, but love your neighbour as yourself.' **(Leviticus 19:18, NIV)**

 'And if they incline to peace, then incline to it [also] and rely upon God. Indeed, it is He who is the Hearing, the Knowing.' **(Surah 8:61)**

Interfaith dialogue (positive interaction between different religious groups and traditions) is a good stepping stone to peace. It allows people to air their views and resolve conflict.

Religious Teachings

Christians, Jews and Muslims all have a duty to protect God's creations and promote peace.

Christians look to the teachings of the Bible and of Jesus Christ on the importance of peace. Striving for justice is seen as a way to end conflict, as violence can often be a response to injustice.

Jesus was a peacemaker who taught his disciples to promote peace and community-making:

'Blessed are the peacemakers, for they will be called children of God.' **(Matthew 5:9, NIV)**

Peace is central to the Jewish concept of tikkun olam; for the world to be healed, there must be peace. Although Judaism teaches that justice is important, and that war is sometimes necessary, the Messianic prophesies envisage a 'golden age' where there is no longer any need for conflict.

The word 'shalom' means 'peace' and 'completeness', emphasising its importance in Judaism.

'On three things the world stands: on judgement, on truth and on peace.' **(Pirkei Avot 1:18)**

Muslims feel a duty to uphold the principles of justice to ensure equality under Sharia law.

While Islam teaches that it is sometimes necessary to go to war in order to oppose injustice and protect Islam, peace is always preferable. Muhammad's example of forgiving his Meccan enemies after the suffering they inflicted on him demonstrates Islam's belief in peace and forgiveness.

'It is He who sent down tranquillity into the hearts of the believers that they would increase in faith along with their [present] faith.' **(Surah 48:4)**

daydream EDUCATION

Peace Organisations and Victims of War

There are various organisations that promote peace, reconciliation, and offer support to victims of war. The United Nations (UN) was formed in 1945, after the Second World War, with one central mission: to maintain international peace and security. It works to prevent and resolve conflict and to ensure lasting peace.

Religious Teachings

There are also many religious organisations that work to promote peace and help victims of war.

✝ Christianity

Helping those in need is important in Christianity, as demonstrated in the parable of the Good Samaritan. Christian organisations that work for peace and help war victims include:

Pax Christi

Pax Christi is a Catholic organisation. It works to create a world of peace by opposing war and violence. It does this by:

- Campaigning against military spending, the arms trade and nuclear weapons
- Helping to promote a culture of peace amongst young people
- Encouraging governments to resolve conflicts peacefully through discussion

CAFOD

CAFOD is a Christian organisation that provides aid in countries affected by war and natural disasters. It does this by:

- Campaigning for justice where government decisions have damaged poor communities
- Encouraging groups in conflict to reconcile
- Rehabilitating, educating and supporting children who have fought as child soldiers
- Providing emergency aid to war refugees

✡ Judaism

The Talmud teaches *'kol yisrael arevim zeh bazeh'* – the idea that the whole Jewish community is responsible for one another. This forms the basis of Jewish charities, including:

The Jewish Peace Fellowship

The Jewish Peace Fellowship was set up in 1941 to support conscientious objectors to war. Today it promotes non-violence by:

- Encouraging governments to resolve conflicts peacefully through discussion, e.g. in Israel and Palestine
- Actively opposing capital punishment

World Jewish Relief

World Jewish Relief started in 1933 to rescue Jews from persecution in Germany. Today it helps those in poverty and provides relief by:

- Providing people in poverty with the means to help themselves by finding work
- Supporting survivors of the Holocaust
- Providing aid and long-term relief in a crisis

☾ Islam

Charity is given discreetly by Muslims to seek forgiveness from Allah. This forms one of the five pillars of Islam: **Zakah**, which amounts to 2.5% of annual savings. Muslim charities include:

Muslim Aid

Muslim Aid was set up in 1985 in response to the famine in Ethiopia. Today it strives to help the poor overcome suffering by:

- Providing aid to war-affected communities
- Providing access to clean drinking water
- Providing education

Muslim Peace Fellowship

The Muslim Peace Fellowship started in 1994 and works to promote world peace and non-violence in the name of Islam by:

- Working against injustice
- Developing nonviolent strategies for the redress of wrongs
- Reaching out to people of other religions to further mutual understanding and respect

daydream
EDUCATION

Weapons of Mass Destruction

A weapon of mass destruction (WMD) is any nuclear, biological or chemical weapon that can cause widespread devastation and loss of life. The use of chemical and biological weapons is banned.

There are two types of nuclear weapons:

Those that depend on fission (splitting atoms): **e.g. atomic bombs**	Those that depend on fusion (joining atoms): **e.g. hydrogen bombs**

WMDs are indiscriminate. This means that they kill both innocent civilians and combatants.

Which Countries Possess Nuclear Weapons?

According to the Arms Control Association, there are nine countries in possession of nuclear weapons (2017): The United States, Russia, The United Kingdom, France, China, India, Pakistan, North Korea and Israel, although Israel has neither denied nor confirmed its possession of nuclear weapons.

Arguments For and Against Nuclear Weapons

There is great debate over whether countries should be allowed to possess nuclear weapons.

For

Some people see nuclear weapons as an effective deterrent to war, helping to ensure peace and preventing further wars.

Those who argue from a **utilitarian** standpoint say that the benefits of using nuclear weapons can sometimes outweigh the negatives of not using them. For example, nuclear weapons can bring a war to its end early, thus preventing further suffering and bloodshed.

Countries that have nuclear weapons may not want to attack each other, as they could risk having their own country destroyed by the other. This is known as **mutually assured destruction (MAD)**.

Against

Many people believe that the devastation and loss of life caused by nuclear weapons goes against the sanctity of life and can never be justified.

Nuclear weapons are costly, and some believe this money could be better spent on health care, aid and other vital services.

There is always the risk of **nuclear proliferation**; that is, they could fall into the hands of those not recognised as agreed 'nuclear weapon states'.

Many religions teach the importance of caring for God's earth and his creatures. Nuclear weapons would destroy the creations that humans should care for.

daydream EDUCATION

Religious Teachings

The huge loss of civilian life and widespread destruction makes the use of nuclear weapons abhorrent to most religious believers.

Christianity

Christianity emphasises the importance of peace through the Bible and through Jesus's teachings. Most Christians are against the use of WMDs as it contradicts these teachings and conflicts with the principles of the just war theory. However, some Christians see WMDs as a necessary deterrent that help maintain peace and prevent future wars.

Judaism

In principle, Jewish teachings conflict with the idea of WMDs. In the Talmud, it states that any action that would harm more than one-sixth of fighting forces is prohibited. Therefore, as WMDs would likely harm more than this number, many Jews oppose their use.

Under Jewish law, it is permissible, however, to threaten to use WMDs as a way of preventing attack. This is seen as the same as telling a lie to protect the life of an innocent person.

Islam

Islam promotes the idea of living a peaceful existence, and if war is unavoidable, then it should always be carried out fairly and without overstepping the mark:

'Fight in the way of God those who fight you but do not transgress. Indeed, God does not like transgressors.' **(Surah 2:190)**

Many Muslims believe that WMDs contradict Islamic teachings on not harming innocent people and damaging the environment. However, Islamic beliefs on using WMDs in retaliation are mixed.

daydream
EDUCATION

Peace & Conflict

What Is...

Peace?

Peace is often defined as 'freedom from violence or conflict'. However, many people believe that it is more than this, involving justice and a commitment to understanding and learning from others.

Justice?

Justice is the protection of rights and punishment of wrongs to maintain fairness in society.

Forgiveness?

Forgiveness involves the release of feelings of resentment toward someone or something that has harmed you, regardless of whether it is deserved or not.

Reconciliation?

Reconciliation is the restoration of peaceful relations after a period of conflict.

Violence & Conflict

Violence is the use of physical force to hurt, damage or kill. According to the World Health Organization (WHO), violence accounts for 1.4 million deaths every year. Forms of violence include:

Violent Protest	Protests are organised public demonstrations to express objection to a course of action. Protests can be carried out peacefully, but if people feel they are being ignored, they may resort to force.
Terrorism	Terrorism is the use of violence in order to achieve political, religious or ideological aims. In 2017, the Manchester Arena was bombed in a terrorist attack that killed 22 people.
War	War is a state of armed conflict between countries, states or societies. When conflict occurs between groups of people within one country, this is known as civil war.

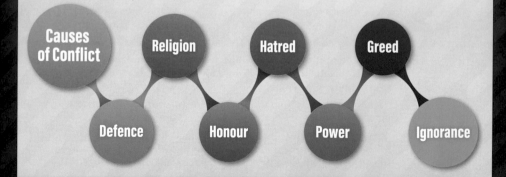

Causes of Conflict — Religion — Hatred — Greed — Defence — Honour — Power — Ignorance

daydream
EDUCATION

The Just War Theory

Christianity, Judaism and Islam all teach that war is not ideal, although it is sometimes unavoidable. A just war is one that is fought for what people believe to be the right reasons.

The just war theory was developed by the Christian theologians St Augustine and St Thomas Aquinas. It states that war is only legitimate if it follows the conditions:

The war must be declared by a lawful authority.	The war must be fought to bring about good.	No harm should be caused to civilians.	There must be a good chance of success.

The war must be for a just cause.	Excessive force should not be used.	War must be the last resort.

The just war theory aims to help people decide whether going to war is the right and just thing to do. It does not justify wars but aims to prevent them by making conflict a last resort.

Holy War

A holy war is a war fought in support of a religious cause, often declared by a religious leader. It is believed that those who fight in holy wars will gain spiritual reward.

Examples of holy wars can be found throughout history, with war being mentioned in the Bible, the Tanakh and the Qur'an. The Crusades and the Battle of Badr are examples of holy wars.

Atheists and humanists are against holy wars as they believe that a war cannot be justifiable as God doesn't exist.

Pacifism

Pacifism is the belief that war and violence are unjustifiable and that disputes should be settled peacefully without violence.

Pacifists advocate peace but also believe that it is important to fight non-violently against injustice.

Gandhi, Aung San Suu Kyi, Martin Luther King and Mother Teresa are well-known pacifists who have promoted peaceful, non-violent protest. Many, such as Gandhi and King, have lost their lives in the struggle for justice.

Martin Luther King

daydream
EDUCATION

No religion actively promotes war and violence. Some terrorist extremists differ on this but do not follow the traditional rules on warfare taught by their religion. However, most religions accept that sometimes war is necessary as a last resort.

Christianity

Christianity aims to promote a peaceful world where justice flourishes and people live in harmony. Some Christians believe that war may however be the only way to achieve this, but only as a last resort and if it meets the conditions of the just war theory.

'In order for a war to be just, three things are necessary. First, the authority of the Sovereign... Secondly, a just cause... Thirdly, a rightful intention.'
(St Thomas Aquinas)

Judaism

In Judaism, there are three types of war:

Milchemet Mitzvah

An 'obligatory' holy war commanded by God.

Milchemet Reshut

An 'optional' war that occurs when all other attempts at peace have failed; a war of last resort.

Pre-emptive war

To attack first when under imminent threat of attack: *'If a person intends to kill you, be first to kill him.'* **(Talmud)**

Islam

In Islam, war is sometimes considered necessary: *'Fight in the cause of God against those who fight you but do not transgress limits.'* **(Surah 2:190)**. Jihad means the 'struggle' or 'fight' for Allah. There are two types of jihad:

Greater Jihad

The personal struggle to follow the teachings of Allah.

Lesser Jihad

The struggle to defend Islam (similar to the concept of holy war).

Jihad is a struggle to improve the world and build a good Muslim society; war is seen as a last resort. It is only justified under certain conditions:

It must only be fought in defence.
Civilians must not be harmed.
Holy buildings must not be damaged.
Crops must be left alone.
There must be fair treatment of war prisoners.

It is a duty for Muslims to fight if a just leader declares war.

daydream
EDUCATION

Crime

Why do people commit crimes?

- Lack of education
- Jealousy
- Upbringing
- Poverty
- Opposition to unjust laws
- Greed

- Mental / physical instability
- Addiction
- Desperation
- Survival
- Peer / family pressure
- Hatred and prejudice

Religious Teachings

Most religions have their own laws that followers must adhere to. However, religious law sometimes conflicts with state law and this can cause problems. In such circumstances, people need to use both their conscience and personal conviction to follow the right path.

Christianity

Christians believe that they should follow all laws except those which are unfair; however, these must be opposed in the most peaceful way possible. Murder and theft, both of which breach the Ten Commandments from the book of Exodus, are considered particularly evil.

Hate crime (crime committed because of prejudice) goes against the teaching of 'love thy neighbour' in the parable of the Good Samaritan.

'You shall not murder.' **(Exodus 20:13, NIV)**

Judaism

Judaism teaches that murder and theft are not allowed under the Ten Commandments. Jews are taught to follow the law but not to obey unjust laws. There are examples in both the Bible and in recent times of Jews ignoring laws in order to do what is right; for example, during the Nazi rule in Germany, many Jews fled persecution despite this being illegal.

'You shall not steal.' **(Exodus 20:15, NIV)**

Islam

Muslims believe that laws should be followed; their own set of laws is called Sharia law. In Sharia law, crimes against others are forgivable, but crimes against Allah are not. Muslims oppose breaking the law as they believe Allah will judge those who do so on the Day of Judgement. There are strict punishments for anybody who breaks Sharia law. Often in Islamic countries, religious and secular laws are one and the same.

'O you who have believed, do not consume one another's wealth unjustly but only [in lawful] business by mutual consent. And do not kill yourselves [or one another]. Indeed, God is to you ever Merciful.'

(Surah 4:29)

Punishment

What is Punishment?

In order for society to work and for there to be justice, most people believe that rules are needed. If the rules are broken, then there should be suitable punishments in place.

Can you ever really put right your wrongs? What about murder?

Vindication: Apply suitable punishments to help enforce the law.

Protection: Protect society from danger.

Given the high reoffending rates, is it not better to lock criminals up and throw away the key?

Are punishments severe enough? Should criminals keep their human rights?

Reparation: Compensate society for criminal activity.

Aims of Punishment

Deterrent: Discourage people from committing crimes.

If deterrents work, why is there still crime?

Is education really punishment?

Reform: Educate and reform the criminal.

Retribution: Make the criminal pay for his/her crime.

Do two wrongs make a right? Is the person enforcing the punishment as bad as the criminal?

Types of Punishment

Different types of punishment are designed to meet different aims. For example:

Capital Punishment (Death)

Compulsory Rehabilitation	Corporal (Physical) Punishment

Probation	Young Offenders Institute	Imprisonment

Fine	ASBO	Tagging	Community Service

Retribution	**Deterrence**	**Reformation**
Capital punishment, corporal punishment, fines, community service	Capital punishment, corporal punishment, imprisonment, electronic tagging, ASBO	Compulsory rehabilitation, community service, imprisonment, probation

daydream
EDUCATION

Religious Teachings

Christianity, Judaism and Islam all teach that punishment is important for the purposes of justice, but that human rights are also important for both victims of crime and for criminals. Everyone has the right to a fair trial.

✝ Christianity

Christians try to follow the example of Jesus Christ, whose teachings demonstrate the importance of love and forgiveness, and of withholding the judgement of others.

'Why do you look at the speck of sawdust in your brother's eye and pay no attention to the plank in your own eye?' **(Matthew 7:3, NIV)**

Christians believe that God will judge all people. Those who have sinned (broken holy laws such as the Ten Commandments) will be punished by God, and those who have committed secular crimes will be punished by man.

Most Christians believe that punishments are needed, but they also believe that criminals should be treated with fairness and respect. Most Christians oppose capital punishment. However, some believe the Old Testament supports it:
'Whoever sheds human blood, by humans shall their blood be shed; for in the image of God has God made mankind.' **(Genesis 9:6, NIV)**

✡ Judaism

Punishment and justice are important in Judaism, but it is also important that criminals are treated fairly. Jews must follow the 613 mitzvot (commandments) outlined in the Torah as well as abiding by state law.

'Hate evil, love good; maintain justice in the courts.' **(Amos 5:15, NIV)**

Jews believe that punishments should be of a similar level to the crime committed: *'eye for eye, tooth for tooth, hand for hand, foot for foot'* **(Exodus 21:24, NIV)**. However, most Jews oppose the death penalty, believing that the penalties outlined in the Torah violate human rights.

Repentance and forgiveness are important in Judaism; they form the two key elements of teshuvah ('return', from sin to righteousness). Helping people reform helps to make the world a better place and is the basis of tikkun olam.

☾ Islam

Justice is an important theme in Islam. Muslims believe that actions against Sharia law are crimes against God and fair punishment is required to restore justice in society. They also believe Allah will punish wrongdoers on the Day of Judgement.

'Know that God is severe in penalty and that God is Forgiving and Merciful.' **(Surah 5:98)**

Many Muslims believe that crimes must be met with punishments of equal severity to the crime for justice to be done, but only after a fair trial has been carried out in a Sharia court. Some punishments from Sharia law are meant to be carried out in public to deter others from the same crime. However, some people think that these punishments are often too severe.

Muslims are taught that Allah is merciful and allows victims to pardon criminals for their actions. By giving criminals the chance to reform, the person who has shown forgiveness will be rewarded in the afterlife: *'But whoever gives [up his right as] charity, it is an expiation for him. And whoever does not judge by what God has revealed – then it is those who are the wrongdoers [i.e. the unjust].'* **(Surah 5:45)**

The Death Penalty

The death penalty, also known as capital punishment, is the execution of a condemned criminal.

Although the death penalty has been abolished in many countries, it remains in use in some (even for minor crimes such as theft). Methods of execution include lethal injection, the electric chair, hanging, decapitation and stoning.

For Capital Punishment

It is a scary deterrent to crime.

The criminal cannot reoffend.

It provides retribution and reparation for victims of crime and their families.

Against Capital Punishment

It is not a deterrent as crimes are often committed in the heat of the moment.

It provides no chance of reform.

Innocent people could be executed.

All human life is special and should not be taken away under any circumstance.

Amnesty International is an organisation that defends human rights, particularly the right to life and freedom from torture. It believes that corporal and capital punishment are wrong.

Religious Teachings

The death penalty is a controversial issue in religion. While many people are against the death penalty and see it as inhumane, others believe it is justifiable as a punishment for murder.

Christianity

Some fundamentalist Christians believe the death penalty is justified: *'eye for eye, tooth for tooth, hand for hand, foot for foot'* (**Exodus 21:24, NIV**). However, the Ten Commandments forbid killing: *'You shall not murder.'* (**Exodus 20:13, NIV**).

Jesus taught his followers to forgive and show mercy as opposed to seeking vengeance, so many Christians believe that the death penalty is wrong and does not give the offender a chance to reform.

Judaism

In Judaism, the death penalty is allowed for some crimes, including murder: *'Whoever sheds human blood, by humans shall their blood be shed; for in the image of God has God made mankind.'* (**Genesis 9:6, NIV**).

Judaism also teaches that life is sacred and only God may choose when a person is born and dies. The Torah puts so many restrictions on the death penalty that it is now hard for Jews to justify. The death penalty is still used in Israel, but is reserved only for the most extreme cases of war crimes.

Islam

The death penalty is allowed in Islamic Sharia law for crimes such as adultery, murder and apostasy. However, families of murder victims are encouraged to accept compensation instead of insisting on the death penalty.

Muslims also believe that all human life is given by Allah, and only Allah decides how long each person will live: *'And it is not [possible] for one to die except by permission of God at a decree determined.'* (**Surah 3:145**).

daydream
EDUCATION

Good, Evil & Suffering

Christianity, Islam and Judaism all teach that people should try to live good lives and avoid causing suffering (pain or distress) to others. Although religions differ in their teachings of evil, most agree that any **action** that is contrary to the character or will of God is considered evil.

There are two types of evil:

- **moral evil** – human actions which are morally wrong, such as murder or theft

- **natural evil** – natural disasters, such as earthquakes or volcanoes

Most religions are against needless suffering. However, some believe that suffering is God's way of testing people or that it is a punishment for past sins. It is the duty of all people to forgive rather than to judge; if a person does wrong, they are to be suitably punished and then forgiven.

✝ Christianity

Christians believe that they should do good deeds in order to achieve salvation. They believe that much of evil is caused by free will and the actions of humans. Christianity is strongly influenced by the example Jesus set of showing love to others:

"Even if they sin against you seven times in a day and seven times come back to you saying 'I repent,' you must forgive them." **(Luke 17:4, NIV)**

Forgiveness is the most loving thing a Christian can do to someone who has wronged them. The Lord's Prayer teaches Christians to ask for forgiveness for wrongdoings and to forgive others.

✡ Judaism

Jews believe that much of the world's evil is caused by humans who abuse the free will given to them by God. Jews see God as merciful. They believe that they should follow His example and forgive any sins committed if the offender shows regret for what he/she has done.

'Do not hate a fellow Israelite in your heart. Rebuke your neighbour frankly so you will not share in their guilt.' **(Leviticus 19:17, NIV)**

☪ Islam

Muslims believe that Shaytan (the devil) influences people to do evil and that those who commit evil will be punished by Allah. Allah will forgive anything apart from the sin of **shirk** (giving godlike attributes to others).

'...whoever pardons and makes reconciliation – his reward is due from God.' **(Surah 42:40)**

Muslims are permitted to seek retribution, but this is not encouraged, as they believe all will be judged by Allah on the Day of Judgement. It is preferable to show mercy and to forgive others.

Atheists do not believe that God causes suffering; they believe it is proof that God doesn't exist. They say that no loving God would let his creations struggle through pain.

daydream EDUCATION

Human Rights

Right to equality and freedom 	**Right to life – to be free and safe**	**Freedom from slavery**	**Right to use the law**	**Right to be protected by the law**

Rights and freedoms cannot be destroyed

The Universal Declaration of Human Rights

Human rights are rights inherent to all human beings, regardless of nationality, place of residence, sex, national or ethnic origin, colour, religion, language, or any other status. All people are equally entitled to our human rights without discrimination. These rights are all interrelated, interdependent and indivisible.

All forms of discrimination violate the first two articles of the UN's Universal Declaration of Human Rights:

Article 1: 'All human beings are born free and equal in dignity and rights. They are endowed with reason and conscience and should act towards one another in a spirit of brotherhood.'

Article 2: 'Everyone is entitled to all the rights and freedoms set forth in this Declaration, without distinction of any kind, such as race, colour, sex, language, religion, political or other opinion, national or social origin, property, birth or other status.'

Right to a fair public hearing or trial

Right to privacy

Right to asylum

Right to own property

Rights and freedoms must be respected

Right to an education

Right to democracy

Right to marriage and family

Right to an adequate living standard

Freedom of belief and religion

Right to rest and leisure

Right to social security

daydream EDUCATION

In 1945, after the Second World War, 51 nations joined together and vowed to never allow such a conflict to occur again. This group of nations established the United Nations (UN) to promote and encourage respect for fundamental human rights and freedoms. On 10 December 1948, the UN adopted the Universal Declaration of Human Rights, a list of rights to which all people are entitled. Today there are over 190 UN member states that continue to fight for 'dignity and justice for all'.

There are currently 30 rights in the Universal Declaration of Human Rights. However, some believe that more rights need to be added.

Religious Views on Human Rights

Christians, Jews and Muslims support human rights as they all protect the lives of humans and the right to practise their religions freely. They also support the rights to fairness, equality and the rule of law supported by all religions.

To support human rights, they are prepared to protest against unfairness and unjust laws. Muslims show particular support for those rights which are also present in Sharia Law and which are focused on justice.

'There is neither Jew nor Gentile, neither slave nor free, nor is there male and female, for you are all one in Christ Jesus.'
(Galatians 3:28, NIV)

'That which is hateful to you, do not do to your fellow.'
(Shabbat 31a)

'O you who have believed, be persistently standing firm in justice, witnesses for God...'
(Surah 4:135)

Religious Freedom

Religious freedom is a complex issue for religious believers, as they have to balance their belief that their religion is the one true religion with the idea of treating everyone as equals.

Christianity

The Christian teaching 'love your neighbour' suggests that Christians should show love to all others, including those of different creeds (faiths) and races. They believe that they should spread the word of their religion while still respecting others' beliefs.

Judaism

Jews are taught to tolerate the beliefs of others, even though they may not necessarily agree with them. They believe that Judaism is the only true faith but have had a long cultural history of co-existing with other religions and supporting religious freedom, especially as they have been persecuted by others in the past.

Islam

Muslims acknowledge the diverse nature of faith but believe that **shirk** (attributing godlike qualities) to anything other than Allah is an unforgivable sin. Leaving Islam to convert to another religion or become an atheist is known as apostasy, and is also unforgivable. However, they believe in having the freedom to follow their own religion and allowing people of other faiths to do the same.

Prejudice & Discrimination

Types of Prejudice and Discrimination

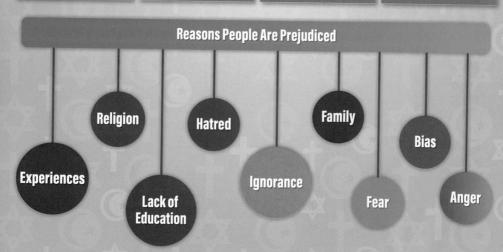

Prejudice
To judge people before you know them and to think negatively about them

Discrimination
To treat people differently and badly based on prejudices

Positive Discrimination
To help people who are usually overlooked

Racism
To treat people differently because of their race

Sexism
To treat people differently because of their gender

Ableism
To treat people who have a disability differently to able-bodied people

Xenophobia
Fear or hatred of foreigners

Homophobia
Fear or hatred of homosexuality

Anti-Semitism
Fear or hatred of Jews

Religious Discrimination
To treat people differently because of their religious beliefs or lack of religious beliefs

Ageism
To treat people differently because of their age

Classism
To treat people differently because of their social class

Reasons People Are Prejudiced

- Experiences
- Religion
- Lack of Education
- Hatred
- Ignorance
- Family
- Fear
- Bias
- Anger

daydream EDUCATION

Religious Attitudes Towards Prejudice and Discrimination

Religion generally teaches that all forms of negative discrimination are wrong. It puts great emphasis on treating all humans with respect and dignity purely because they are human. All humans are unique and have their own identity. This must be celebrated, not punished. All humans are part of God's creation and have the right to be treated equally with fairness and justice.

Christianity

'A new command I give you: Love one another. As I have loved you, so you must love one another.' **(John 13:34, NIV)**

There are many teachings from the Bible that focus on the idea of showing God's love to one's neighbours, such as the Parable of the Good Samaritan. Christians believe that all of mankind is their neighbour, and that they should extend help, support and love to all, regardless of race or religion.

Judaism

'When a foreigner resides among you in your land, do not mistreat them. The foreigner residing among you must be treated as your native-born. Love them as yourself...' **(Leviticus 19:33-34, NIV)**

Although Jews believe that they are the chosen people of God, this does not mean that they believe they are better than others; this is just the role given to them by God. They believe that God created all people, that everyone is an equal and, as such, should be treated with love.

Islam

'All people are equal... as the teeth of a comb. No Arab can claim merit over a non-Arab, nor a white person over a black person, nor a male over a female.' **(Hadith)**

Islam not only teaches its followers to treat others equally, but to also celebrate people's differences as part of the beauty of Allah's creation. Muhammad himself had followers and converts from other nations, and this demonstrates a personal example of treating other races well.

The Universal Declaration of Human Rights

Human rights are rights inherent to all human beings, regardless of nationality, place of residence, sex, national or ethnic origin, colour, religion, language or any other status. All people are equally entitled to human rights without discrimination. These rights are all interrelated, interdependent and indivisible.

All forms of discrimination violate the first two articles of the United Nations' Universal Declaration of Human Rights:

Article 1: 'All human beings are born free and equal in dignity and rights. They are endowed with reason and conscience and should act towards one another in a spirit of brotherhood.'

Article 2: 'Everyone is entitled to all the rights and freedoms set forth in this Declaration, without distinction of any kind, such as race, colour, sex, language, religion, political or other opinion, national or social origin, property, birth or other status.'

Key Figures

Many people from around the world, such as Martin Luther King, Emmeline Pankhurst and Gandhi, have gone to great lengths to put a stop to discrimination. They have understood that human rights matter. People should not live in a world in which they are labelled. People should all be free to make their own choices without fear of being persecuted, harassed and victimised by others.

daydream EDUCATION

87

Discrimination

Homosexual Discrimination

Christianity, Judaism and Islam traditionally teach that homosexuality is wrong, but attitudes have changed over recent years.

Christianity

Christians, particularly Catholic Christians, have traditionally taught that having homosexual relations is wrong: *'Do not have sexual relations with a man as one does with a woman; that is detestable.'* **(Leviticus 18:22, NIV).**

However, some Christians believe that this contradicts Jesus's teachings to 'love your neighbour' and believe that everyone should be treated well, regardless of sexuality.

Judaism

Jews, particularly Orthodox Jews, generally see homosexual relations as a sin. The Torah forbids homosexual acts (Mishkav Zakhar). However, Liberal and some Reform Jews are more accepting of homosexuality and now allow homosexual people to become rabbis.

Islam

Many Muslims believe that the Qur'an forbids homosexuality. In modern Britain, Muslims are generally tolerant of it, but most would not encourage it amongst their believers.

Gender Discrimination

Most religions teach that all men and women are equal and should be treated equally. However, most religions also view men and women as different, with different roles to play.

Each role is of equal importance. Women are traditionally expected to look after the home and the children, whereas men are expected to go out and work.

More recently however, there has been greater acceptance of female ministers and rabbis, and more prominent roles for Muslim women in the mosque.

daydream
EDUCATION

Racial Discrimination

Racial discrimination has led to many injustices in society, including the slave trade. Racial discrimination continues to pose problems in society today, creating social tension and leading to an increase in crime and violence.

Christians, Jews and Muslims all believe in working towards racial harmony, encouraging all races to live together with respect and understanding.

Christianity

'There is neither Jew nor Gentile, neither slave nor free, nor is there male and female, for you are all one in Christ Jesus.' **(Galatians 3:28, NIV)**

Christians are taught to follow the example of Jesus Christ, who treated all people equally. They believe that following Jesus unites them as part of one Church and one community, regardless of race or nationality.

Judaism

'When a foreigner resides among you in your land, do not mistreat them. The foreigner residing among you must be treated as your native-born. Love them as yourself, for you were foreigners in Egypt. I am the Lord your God.' **(Leviticus 19:33-34, NIV)**

Judaism teaches that all races should be treated equally. Jews have faced anti-Semitism (prejudice against Jews) throughout history; for example, during the Holocaust. This mistreatment means that Jews are acutely aware of the harshness of discrimination. The Jewish Council for Racial Equality promotes equality for refugees and asylum seekers.

Islam

'O mankind, indeed We have created you from male and female and made you peoples and tribes that you may know one another. Indeed, the most noble of you in the sight of Allah is the most righteous of you.' **(Surah 49:13)**

Muslims believe that Allah created all humans as equals, though not the same, and as such all deserve equal respect. Prophet Muhammad in his last sermon also taught that all people should be treated equally, regardless of race or religion.

Key Figures Against Racial Prejudice and Discrimination

People of different religions have long fought for racial equality and justice for all.

Rosa Parks (1913-2005)

Rosa Parks, a Christian, started the Montgomery Bus Boycott in 1955 when she refused to give up her seat to a white person. She was a key figure in the Civil Rights Movement for racial equality.

Harry Schwarz (1924-2010)

Harry Schwarz, a Jewish South African lawyer and politician, was best known for his position as opposition leader against apartheid (racial discrimination) in South Africa.

Muhammad Ali (1942-2016)

Muhammad Ali was a Muslim boxer and activist who campaigned against the Vietnam War, racism and Islamophobia. He earned the Presidential Medal of Freedom in 2005.

Social Justice

Social justice involves equality for all, including the equal distribution of wealth.

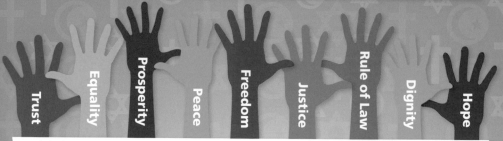

Trust · Equality · Prosperity · Peace · Freedom · Justice · Rule of Law · Dignity · Hope

Christianity, Judaism and Islam all teach the importance of equality, tolerance and fairness for all, and social justice is an important concept in all three religions.

Christianity
'He has shown you, O mortal, what is good. And what does the Lord require of you? To act justly and to love mercy and to walk humbly with your God.'

(Micah 6:8, NIV)

Judaism
'Learn to do right; seek justice. Defend the oppressed. Take up the cause of the fatherless; plead the case of the widow… Zion will be delivered with justice, her penitent ones with righteousness.'

(Isaiah 1:17, 1:27, NIV)

Islam
'Indeed, God orders justice and good conduct and giving to relatives and forbids immorality and bad conduct and oppression.'

(Surah 16:90)

Wealth and Poverty

Wealth measures the value of all the assets of worth owned by a person, community, company or country. In the UK, and globally, wealth is not distributed evenly, and the gap between the richest and poorest is getting bigger, leading to great wealth inequality.

Aggregate total wealth in UK 2014–2016

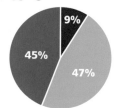

9%
45%
47%

Least wealthy:
1% to 50%

Middle wealth:
51% to 90%

Wealthiest 10%

The graph opposite shows how the richest 10% of the UK's population has almost half of the UK's total wealth.

daydream EDUCATION

Lack of skills

Low pay

Cost of living

Causes of Poverty

Natural disasters

Unemployment

War

Debt

People Trafficking

Some people who are trying to escape poverty fall victim to people trafficking. Often, they are promised a better life in another place where they can work and earn a better living. However, when they arrive, they are then forced to work in terrible conditions.

Excessive Interest on Loans

Some people take out payday loans to cover urgent costs, such as an unexpected car repair. However, interest rates can go up to thousands of percent, making it extremely difficult to pay back the money borrowed. This in turn worsens debt, pushing the borrower further into poverty.

Unfair Pay

Many people in the UK have poorly-paid jobs, either because better-paid jobs are not available, or they lack the skills to perform such jobs. Many argue that both the National Minimum Wage and National Living Wage are not enough to live on.

Religious Responses to Poverty

Helping those in poverty is a key part of Christianity, Judaism and Islam.
All three religions place importance on charity to help the poor and needy.

Christianity

Christianity emphasises that those in need should be helped, regardless of their faith. Christian charities such as Christian Aid, CAFOD and Tearfund work to relieve the impact of poverty. These charities also work to tackle a range of other issues. These include the promotion of equal rights for women and girls worldwide, and pushing political leaders to deal with climate change.

"What good is it, my brothers and sisters, if someone claims to have faith but has no deeds? Can such faith save them? Suppose a brother or a sister is without clothes and daily food. If one of you says to them, 'Go in peace; keep warm and well fed,' but does nothing about their physical needs, what good is it?" **(James 2:14-16, NIV)**

For Christians, part of reaching heaven is through seeking salvation through good works; in other words, charity for the poor will guarantee them a place in the afterlife.

Judaism

Jews are taught to support each other financially by giving others the means to help themselves. They also believe that they should never charge other Jews interest on money they have lent; by not charging interest, this allows others to better themselves without being faced with unfair repayments. However, this does not apply to the money lent to non-Jews.

'You may charge a foreigner interest, but not a fellow Israelite.' **(Deuteronomy 23:20, NIV)**

Jews try to help others so they have the means to escape poverty, but not to depend upon aid. Part of tikkun olam is to help others in need.

Islam

Islam teaches that all wealth belongs to Allah and that it is cleansed through zakah (financial aid). Zakah is one of the Five Pillars of Islam and is an important duty for Muslims. Writing off debt for those who owe money is seen as a charitable act which will be looked upon favourably by Allah.

'He who eats and drinks while his brother goes hungry is not one of us.' **(Hadith)**

It is believed that by helping others in need, Muslims will be rewarded by Allah in the afterlife.

The Early Ministry of Jesus

John the Baptist (Mark 1:1-8)

Mark's Gospel begins with the story of John the Baptist; the messenger sent by God to prepare the world for the coming **Messiah*** (Jesus).

'I will send my messenger ahead of you, who will prepare your way' **(Mark 1:2, NIV)**

John baptised people by total submersion in the River Jordan to cleanse them of their sins and enable them to lead good lives following God.

Only those who truly repented were cleansed of sin. John promised that somebody greater than him would come to baptise people with the Holy Spirit; this refers to the long-awaited appearance of the Messiah who will save those who turn to God.

'I baptize you with water, but he will baptize you with the Holy Spirit.' **(Mark 1:8, NIV)**

* The term 'Messiah' was given to the kings of Israel and describes Jesus as the leader and saviour of the Jewish people. This was a title not used by Jesus, but by his followers as part of the 'Messianic Secret'. Jesus's role as the Messiah was only revealed after his death and resurrection.

Jesus's Baptism and Temptation by Satan (Mark 1:9-13)

John baptised Jesus in the River Jordan. After the baptism, Jesus heard a voice telling him that he was the **Son of God***.

"Just as Jesus was coming up out of the water, he saw heaven being torn open and the Spirit descending on him like a dove. And a voice came from heaven: 'You are my Son, whom I love; with you I am well pleased.'" **(Mark 1:10-11, NIV)**.

At the command of the Holy Spirit, Jesus then went into the desert for forty days and nights.

'...he was in the wilderness forty days, being tempted by Satan. He was with the wild animals, and angels attended him.' **(Mark 1:13, NIV)**

In the desert, Jesus resisted temptation; this not only showed his purity and power but also acts as a guide for Christians today.

Jesus proved that temptation can be resisted to lead a good and righteous life.

Christians commemorate his struggle by resisting temptation during Lent.

* Jesus's title as the Son of God shows Jesus's importance through his special relationship with God. The term was also used in the Old Testament to refer to the kings of Israel.

Miracles

Miracles not only form an important part of Jesus's life story, but they also show how powerful he was. His ability to heal, provide for the needy and raise the dead demonstrate his divine nature. For Christians, miracles are proof that Jesus is the Son of God.

The Paralysed Man (Mark 2:1-12)

During Jesus's early ministry, news of his miracles spread quickly, and when he visited the town of Capernaum, a huge crowd of people gathered in a house to learn from him.

Hearing that Jesus was there, four men carried their paralysed friend to the house in the hope that Jesus would heal him. The house was so crowded that they couldn't get in, so they climbed up onto the roof and lowered their friend down to Jesus on a mat.

Jesus was moved by their faith so he forgave the man for his sins. He knew that being paralysed was hard, but not being forgiven was even harder to bear. The people around him were outraged, thinking that Jesus was blaspheming by claiming God's authority to forgive sins.

'Why does this fellow talk like that? He's blaspheming! Who can forgive sins but God alone?' (Mark 2:7, NIV)

Jesus knew in his spirit that the people were outraged so he proved his authority as **Son of Man*** by healing the man, commanding him to get up and go home.

'I tell you, get up, take your mat and go home.' (Mark 2:11, NIV)

Seeing that the man was healed, the crowd were filled with awe and praised God.

* Jesus referred to himself as the Son of Man, which suggests his humanity. It could also describe his divine nature, as shown in Daniel 7:14 '...all nations and peoples of every language worshiped him.' Jesus was both fully human and fully divine.

The Daughter of Jairus (Mark 5:21-24, 35-43)

One day a man named Jairus, a synagogue leader, broke through a crowd that had gathered around Jesus and fell at his feet. He told Jesus that his young daughter was very ill and begged Jesus to heal her. Jesus followed him, accompanied by the crowd.

However, when they arrived at the house it was too late, but Jesus told Jairus to have faith: 'Don't be afraid; just believe.' (Mark 5:36, NIV). He went in to see the girl and told Jairus that she was just sleeping, only to be met with laughter from the people who knew that the girl was dead.

"He took her by the hand and said to her, 'Talitha koum!' (which means 'Little girl, I say to you, get up!')". (Mark 5:41, NIV)

At Jesus's command, the girl stood up and walked around the room. The crowd were amazed, and Jesus told them not to mention what they had witnessed to anyone else.

The story illustrates how having faith in God can make all things possible; even bringing the dead back to life. Jairus kept his faith in the Son of God and so his daughter was healed.

94

The Rejection at Nazareth (Mark 6:1-6)

Despite the praise and adoration that Jesus received for his work, people in his hometown of Nazareth did not believe that he could be the Son of God. When he started teaching at the synagogue, people could only remember Jesus as the carpenter's son and they rejected him.

"'Isn't this the carpenter? Isn't this Mary's son and the brother of James, Joseph, Judas and Simon? Aren't his sisters here with us?' And they took offense at him." (Mark 6:3, NIV)

Jesus was amazed by their lack of faith.

"'...A prophet is not without honor except in his own town, among his relatives and in his own home.' He could not do any miracles there, except lay his hands on a few sick people and heal them. He was amazed at their lack of faith." (Mark 6: 4-6, NIV)

This passage teaches Christians that they must always have faith to receive God's blessings. It also helps people who have been rejected by their families, knowing that Jesus experienced the same sufferings and rejection.

The Feeding of the Five Thousand (Mark 6:30-44)

As Jesus was preaching to a large crowd, he told them to follow him to an isolated place so that they could rest. However, many people who had seen the crowd followed too. Jesus '...had compassion on them, because they were like sheep without a shepherd' (Mark 6:34, NIV) so he began teaching them too.

It had grown late and the people had not eaten, so Jesus instructed his disciples to feed the people in the crowd. His disciples pointed out that they only had five loaves of bread and two fish. Jesus took the bread and loaves, looked up to heaven, gave thanks and broke the loaves.

He managed to distribute this food among 5,000 people with still some left over at the end.

'They all ate and were satisfied, and the disciples picked up twelve basketfuls of broken pieces of bread and fish.' (Mark 6:42-43, NIV)

The story of Jesus feeding the 5,000 is a significant miracle for Christians, having been recorded in all Four Gospels. It teaches Christians to show generosity, empathy and compassion to others. God can help Christians overcome their biggest challenges with whatever little offerings they have. However, they must have faith that God is great and can provide for them.

The story reminds Christians of the Last Supper, where Jesus broke bread with his disciples just before his death; Jesus is the 'bread of life' and can feed Christians' spiritually.

At the end of the miracle, there are 12 baskets of broken bread left (the exact number of Jesus's disciples) emphasising that God provides for those who serve others.

The Later Ministry of Jesus

The events of Jesus's later ministry took place in Jerusalem, where he died and was resurrected.

The Conversation at Caesarea Philippi (Mark 8:27-33)

As Jesus was travelling around Caesarea Philippi, he asked his disciples, *'who do people say I am?'* and they responded, *'Some say John the Baptist; others say Elijah; and still others, one of the prophets.'* **(Mark 8:28, NIV)**. He then asked his disciples who they said he was.

Peter told him, *'You are the Messiah.'* **(Mark 8:29, NIV)**. This is the first time that Jesus is declared the Messiah, and Jesus warned his disciples not to tell anyone*.

*Some people believe that Jesus did not want people to know he was the Messiah because his role would have been misinterpreted and difficult to accept until after his resurrection. This is known as the **Messianic Secret**.

Jesus then predicted his death followed by his resurrection. Peter rebuked Jesus's prediction, refusing to believe that the Messiah could possibly die, and this angered Jesus.

"'Get behind me, Satan!' he said. 'You do not have in mind the concerns of God, but merely human concerns.'" **(Mark 8:33, NIV)**

Peter was looking at things from an earthly perspective, one which tried to divert Jesus away from God's plan for him on the cross. Though Peter did not do this intentionally, it is a reminder of how Satan tried to tempt Jesus during his time in the wilderness.

The Transfiguration of Jesus (Mark 9:2-9)

Jesus went up a high mountain with three of his closest disciples: Peter, James and John. Whilst there, Jesus **transfigured** (changed appearance) before their eyes; his clothes were bathed in a dazzling divine light, and Moses and Elijah appeared before him.

Moses and Elijah are key biblical figures. Moses gave the Jews their basic laws and Elijah was known as the greatest of the prophets. Their appearance in this passage was proof that Jesus was the awaited Messiah whom the law and the prophets spoke of.

The disciples were afraid. They were being shown a glimpse of God's divine kingdom beyond their earthly realm. God then spoke as a voice in the clouds. This reflects back to God speaking of his love for Jesus during the baptism **(Mark 1:9-13)**.

"Then a cloud appeared and covered them, and a voice came from the cloud: 'This is my Son, whom I love. Listen to him!'" **(Mark 9:7, NIV)**

Jesus told his disciples not to speak of the event until after his resurrection.

Jesus Predicts the Passion (Mark 10:32-34)

On the way to Jerusalem with his disciples, Jesus predicted for a third time that he would die and rise again three days later. This is the first time he gives specific detail of his final hours.

'...and the Son of Man will be delivered over to the chief priests and the teachers of the law. They will condemn him to death and will hand him over to the Gentiles, who will mock him and spit on him, flog him and kill him. Three days later he will rise.' **(Mark: 10:33-34, NIV)**

Although Jesus had already foretold his own death, it still came as a devastating shock to his disciples. Later, however, they realised that Jesus's death fulfilled a prophecy and allowed Jesus to save those who believed in him from sin. This sacrifice was a necessary part of God's plan.

daydream EDUCATION

The Request of James and John (Mark 10:35-45)

In this passage, Jesus teaches his disciples an important lesson about serving others. James and John asked Jesus if they could sit at his left and right sides in heaven so that they could take the positions as the most important disciples. Jesus then asked them if they would suffer with him.

"'You don't know what you are asking,' Jesus said. 'Can you drink the cup I drink or be baptized with the baptism I am baptized with?'" **(Mark 10:38, NIV)**

Jesus responded by telling them that their positions were not their own decisions; only God had this power. The behaviour of James and John angered the other disciples, but Jesus called them all together and said: *'...whoever wants to become great among you must be your servant, and whoever wants to be first must be slave of all.'* **(Mark 10:43-44, NIV)**

Jesus lived his life as an example to others of the importance of servitude. He came to Earth to help and heal others, and to pay for humanity's sins through the ultimate sacrifice: his life. Christians today try to serve others through good deeds and charities such as Christian Aid.

Bartimaeus (Mark 10:46-52)

Jesus and his followers were leaving Jericho when they came across a blind man, Bartimaeus, sitting by the roadside and begging. He called out to Jesus. Though the crowd tried to silence him, he persisted.

"Many rebuked him and told him to be quiet, but he shouted all the more, 'Son of David, have mercy on me!'" **(Mark 10:48, NIV)**

Jesus then asked Bartimeus to come to him, so he could hear his request. When Bartimeus requested, *'Rabbi, I want to see'* **(Mark 10:51, NIV)**, Jesus immediately healed him.

Bartimeus showed unwavering faith; not only by addressing Jesus as the Son of David, but also the fact that he continued to call, believing in his heart that Jesus would stop and help him.

For many Christians, this story represents spiritual blindness without Jesus.

The Entry into Jerusalem (Mark 11:1-11)

Jesus rode into Jerusalem on a colt (donkey) which he had ordered his disciples to fetch for him. Although he was entering Jerusalem as the celebrated and awaited Messiah, Jesus did not ride a grand steed as people expected. The donkey reflects Jesus's humble and peaceful nature.

People spread cloaks and branches across Jesus's path as he passed and shouted praises.

"'Hosanna!'
'Blessed is he who comes in the name of the Lord!'
'Blessed is the coming kingdom of our father David!'
'Hosanna in the highest heaven!'"
(Mark 11:9-10, NIV)

Laying cloaks across Jesus's path was a way of showing that he was respected as a king and leader. The chants of 'Hosanna!' are a plea for salvation; people wanted to be saved by the Messiah.

Christians today celebrate Palm Sunday to remember Jesus's triumphant entry into Jerusalem.

The Final Days in Jerusalem

The Last Supper (Mark 14:12-26)

Jesus and his disciples shared a Passover meal together on the night before he was crucified. During the meal, Jesus revealed that one of the twelve disciples would betray him.

 '...Truly I tell you, one of you will betray me - one who is eating with me.' (Mark 14:18)

Jesus shared bread and wine with his disciples. Breaking the bread, he announced that it was his body and passed it around. He then passed around a cup of wine and declared it his blood. The tradition of sharing bread and wine now has significance as part of the Eucharist (Holy Communion).

Some Christians, such as Roman Catholics, believe that the bread and wine literally became Jesus's body and blood; this is known as transubstantiation. Others believe the meaning is purely symbolic.

Jesus says of the wine, *'This is my blood of the covenant'* (Mark 14:24, NIV), marking the start of a new relationship between God and mankind through the death of Christ.

Jesus in Gethsemane (Mark 14:32-52)

In the Garden of Gethsemene, Jesus told his disciples to keep watch while he prayed to God. However, each time he returned, they had fallen asleep. Overwhelmed with sorrow, Jesus knew he was going to die. However, during his prayers he found the strength to submit to God's will.

'Take this cup from me. Yet not what I will, but what you will.' (Mark 14:36, NIV)

As Jesus was speaking with his disciples, Judas (one of his disciples) arrived with an armed crowd to arrest Jesus. He had agreed with them beforehand to reveal Jesus's identity by kissing his cheek. During Jesus's arrest, one of his disciples tried to defend him, cutting off the ear of one of Jesus's accusers. However, Jesus accepted his fate, stating *'...the Scriptures must be fulfilled.'* (Mark 14:49, NIV)

Jesus's distress showed his human nature, whilst his willingness to suffer for mankind showed his dedication to God. His acceptance of his fate sets an example for Christians today to always have faith in God's plan, no matter how difficult this is.

The Trial Before the Jewish Authorities (Mark 14:53-65)

When Jesus was tried by the Jewish authorities, the high priest asked Jesus if he was the Messiah. Jesus replied, 'I am'. This is very important because it was a phrase used by God in the Old Testament and shows that Jesus fully intended to declare his role as the Son of God.

This enraged the authorities and they accused him of blasphemy and *'condemned him as worthy of death.'* (Mark 14:64, NIV). Had Jesus said at any point that he was not the Son of God, he would have been spared. This demonstrates Jesus's unwavering faith, even in the face of persecution.

 daydream EDUCATION

The Trial Before Pilate (Mark 15:1-15)

When brought before the Roman governor, Pontius Pilate, Jesus was asked, *'Are you the king of the Jews?'* Jesus replied, *'You have said so.'* **(Mark 15:2, NIV)**. Jesus did not defend himself.

It was tradition to release a prisoner at Passover and once Pilate realised that Jesus was not a political threat to him, he offered to release him. However, under the influence of the chief priests, the attending crowd demanded that the murderer, Barabbas, be released instead.

Pilate created several opportunities for Jesus to be freed, but the crowd kept shouting, *'Crucify him!'* **(Mark 15:13, NIV)**. As a result, Pilate had Jesus flogged and handed over for crucifixion.

The Crucifixion and Burial (Mark 15:21-47)

Jesus was taken to Golgotha (place of the skull) and put on the cross at 9 am. A sign stated his crime:	*'THE KING OF THE JEWS'* **(Mark 15:26, NIV)**
Passers-by, the crucifiers and the chief priests all mocked Jesus.	*"'...He saved others,'* they said, *'but he can't save himself!'"* **(Mark 15:31, NIV)**

At midday, the skies darkened, and at 3pm Jesus cried out in agony, *'My God, my God, why have you forsaken me?'* **(Mark 15:34, NIV)**. He cried out once more, wordlessly, and breathed his last.

As Jesus died, the temple curtain tore in two to reveal a special room called 'The Holy of Holies' where it was believed God dwelt and which could only be accessed by the high priest. This was symbolic of the divide created between humans and God by sin being broken through Jesus's sacrifice. Now anybody could reach out to God, not just priests.

After witnessing the brutal nature of Jesus's death, a Roman soldier cried out *'Surely this man was the Son of God!'* **(Mark 15:39, NIV)**.

Joseph of Arimathea requested that he take Christ's body so that he could wrap it in linen (a traditional Jewish burial custom) and place it in a tomb made of rock.

The Empty Tomb (Mark 16:1-8)

On the Sunday following Jesus's crucifixion, three women went to his tomb. However, once there, they found that the stone blocking the entrance had moved, and inside the tomb sat a young man dressed in white who told them that Jesus had returned.

"You are looking for Jesus the Nazarene, who was crucified. He has risen! He is not here. See the place where they laid him. But go, tell his disciples and Peter, 'He is going ahead of you into Galilee.'" **(Mark 16:6-7)**

The women were so bewildered and afraid, they fled the tomb and told no one about the encounter. Jesus's resurrection gave hope to his disciples. Jesus defied death, proving he really was the Son of God. However, some people argue that a physical resurrection never really happened:

Jesus only fainted on the cross and was placed in the tomb. He then recovered and left the tomb.	Jesus had been declared dead by the soldiers, Pilate and the women. How could they all be wrong?
Jesus did not rise from the dead. The disciples probably stole the body.	Why would the frightened disciples risk trying to steal the body? If caught, they would have faced the death penalty.
The resurrection was spiritual. Jesus's body itself was not resurrected.	Then how do you explain the accounts which note that a physical body was placed in the tomb only to disappear?

The Kingdom of God

The Kingdom of God can have different meanings to Christians. Parables help Christians to understand the concept.

The Kingdom of God can refer to a time when God will rule supreme and people will live in accordance with God's will. It forms an important part of Jesus's teachings on how the world should be, with people living righteous lives in service to God and to others.

The Kingdom of God can exist in different places and in the hearts and minds of those who follow Jesus. For some, it is a state of being or a way of life, whereas others believe it is a physical place that will come about when Jesus returns to Earth on Judgement Day (**the Second Coming**). On this day, those who have lived righteous lives will be rewarded and those who have sinned will be punished.

Parables of the Kingdom of God

A parable is a simple story used to illustrate a moral or spiritual lesson, as told by Jesus in the Gospels, to help people understand the nature of the Kingdom of God.

Parable of the Sower (Mark 4:1-9, 14-20)

Jesus used the Parable of the Sower to explain the different responses to his teachings. In the story, a sower spreads seeds on to different ground. The sower represents Jesus, the seed is the Word of God and the different types of ground represent different responses to the Word of God.

The **seeds spread on the path** were eaten by birds. The hard path represents someone with a hardened heart that hears the Word of God but does not accept it. The birds are a metaphor for Satan who helps people forget the teaching of God.

The **seeds that fell on stony ground** grew quickly but were scorched by the sun as they had no roots. This represents the people who accept God's Word but give up when things get hard.

The **seeds that fell on thorny ground** were choked by thorns and weeds. This represents the people who accept God's Word but abandon it for distractions such as greed, lust and wealth.

The **seeds that fell on good ground** grew well and flourished. This represents the people who accept God's Word and live their lives by it.

Jesus showed people how their willingness to follow his teachings determined how in touch they would be with the Kingdom of God.

Parable of the Growing Seed (Mark 4:26-29)

In the Parable of the Growing Seed, the Word of God is represented by the seed being sown in a farmer's field. The farmer may not know how the seeds are growing, but he is reassured by the knowledge that growth is happening. They are then ready for him to reap at harvest time.

In the same way, Christians may not understand how God's love is working in the world, but they can be safe in the knowledge that it is.

Jesus says of the parable: *'This is what the kingdom of God is like.'* (**Mark 4:26, NIV**). Like the crops, the Kingdom of God grows until harvest time, and those who have led righteous lives will be accepted into the Kingdom of God on Judgement Day.

Parable Of The Mustard Seed (Mark 4:30-32)

Jesus explains that the Kingdom of God is like a mustard seed; it may start off as the smallest seed, but grows into *'…the largest of all garden plants, with such big branches that the birds can perch in its shade.'* (**Mark 4:32, NIV**).

Like the mustard seed, the Kingdom of God had very small beginnings, consisting of just Jesus and his followers. However, this grew and grew to reach a wide community of people. Some people believe this represents the growth of the Church. The mustard plant offers a place of refuge to the birds, which are symbolic of non-Christians who became attracted to the Christian faith.

Just as the mustard seed was sown in the ground, the Gospel was introduced to people on Earth.

daydream EDUCATION

Jesus and the Children (Mark 10:13-16)

When Jesus was preaching, people would often bring their children to see him. His disciples tried to stop them, but Jesus intervened and welcomed the children.

"'…anyone who will not receive the kingdom of God like a little child will never enter it.' And he took the children in his arms, placed his hands on them and blessed them." **(Mark 10:15-16, NIV)**

This passage is very important as it teaches key messages:

- Children should be seen as an important part of the Christian community. They should be welcomed and taught the ways of the faith.
- The Kingdom of God should be embraced and accepted with a child-like curiosity and joy.

The Rich Man (Mark 10:17-27)

A young rich man desiring eternal life fell to his knees and asked Jesus how he could secure a place in heaven. Jesus reminded him of the Ten Commandments.

'You shall not murder, you shall not commit adultery, you shall not steal, you shall not give false testimony, you shall not defraud, honor your father and mother.' **(Mark 10:19, NIV)**

The rich man assured Jesus that he already followed the Ten Commandments. Jesus told him to sell all that he owned and to follow him. The man, unable to sacrifice his wealth, walked away sadly.

Jesus stated that *'It is easier for a camel to go through the eye of a needle than for someone who is rich to enter the kingdom of God.'* **(Mark 10:25, NIV)**. This means that it is difficult for people with wealth to be saved; material possessions are a distraction from a righteous life.

Some Christians believe this means they should abandon their wealth altogether, whereas others believe they should use their wealth to be charitable and help others in need. However, this is unlikely to work in the modern world as it is no longer possible to live without wealth for survival.

The parables are very clear in showing that greed and excess prevent people from entering the Kingdom of God. Jesus went against the traditional Jewish teaching where riches were seen as a sign of God's favour. He taught Christians to live a spiritual life, worshipping God above money.

The Greatest Commandment (Mark 12:28-34)

"'The most important one…is this…the Lord our God, the Lord is one. Love the Lord your God with all your heart and with all your soul and with all your mind and with all your strength.' The second is this: 'Love your neighbour as yourself.'" **(Mark 12:29-31, NIV)**

When asked by a teacher, Jesus said that the most important of the Ten Commandments is to love God above all else. The second most important is to love others. The first commandment forms part of the Jewish Shema prayer: a declaration of faith in only one God.

The principle of *'love your neighbour'* can be demonstrated through charitable work and in carrying out the evangelistic mission to save others through Jesus's love.

The Old Testament contains a similar principle to love others; however, this only applies to fellow Jews. Jesus taught people to love everyone, regardless of race or beliefs.

Jesus & People Disregarded by Society

Jesus accepted everyone and treated them with love and compassion, including those normally disregarded and excluded by society.

There were many groups of people in 1st century Jewish society who were persecuted by others.

Sinners ▶ Those who broke the law were outcast by Jews.

Gentiles ▶ Jews were not to make contact with non-Jews so as to avoid becoming impure.

The Poor ▶ The poor were marginalised and neglected by Jewish society.

The Sick ▶ The sick were being punished by God so they were isolated from society.

Tax Collectors ▶ Jews who collected taxes for the Romans were seen as traitors and were hated.

Women ▶ Women were subject to male authority.

Jesus broke religious laws to welcome those disregarded by society into the Kingdom of God. Christians are taught to love and forgive everybody, regardless of race, gender or history.

The Man with Leprosy (Mark 1:40-45)

A leper came to Jesus and begged to be cured. Leprosy is a very serious disease which people at the time believed was spread through touching. As a result, lepers were isolated from society.

Jesus was willing to touch the leper to heal him: *'I am willing...be clean!'* (Mark 1:41, NIV). He then told the leper to make the appropriate sacrifices and find a priest to declare him cured of leprosy. He warned the man not to tell anybody about what had just happened. However, the man told everyone he met to spread the news of his miraculous healing.

Christians are taught to help the sick even when there are personal risks. Today, there are many Christian charities that help people affected by serious illness. An example of this is Samaritan's Purse, whose projects have included helping patients during the Ebola crisis.

The Call of Levi (Mark 2:13-17)

Jesus invited the tax collector, Levi, to follow him. Tax collectors worked for Roman forces and were believed to be dishonest and untrustworthy. People did not usually like to associate with them.

Jesus then went to Levi's house to eat with him and the other sinners who were there. This angered some people: *'Why does he eat with tax collectors and sinners?'* (Mark 2:16, NIV)

Jesus responded by telling them that it was important to help those who had sinned.

> *'It is not the healthy who need a doctor, but the sick.*
> *I have not come to call the righteous, but sinners.'* (Mark 2:17, NIV)

Jesus does not judge based on a sinner's past. He teaches others to have mercy and to help past sinners find the path to righteousness. Levi later became one of Jesus's disciples.

The Greek Woman's Daughter (Mark 7:24-30)

A Greek (Syrophoenician) woman asked Jesus to help her daughter who was possessed by a demon. As a woman and a Gentile, the Greek woman was doubly marginalised by society.

Jesus initially refused, explaining that he must help Jews before Gentiles. However, she responded by saying, *'Lord…even the dogs under the table eat the children's crumbs.'* (**Mark 7:28, NIV**). She showed that she not only honoured Jesus's mission, but called him *'Lord'*, a mark of her faith and respect. Jesus saw the woman's faith and healed her daughter.

Throughout his ministry, Jesus helped many Gentiles, some of whom turned to Christianity following his death and resurrection. This story teaches the importance of showing compassion to all.

The Demon-Possessed Boy (Mark 9:14-29)

A man asked Jesus to help his son whom he believed was possessed. He was convulsing and frothing at the mouth. Jesus saw that the man's faith was weak so he rebuked him and the crowd, saying that anything was possible for those with faith. The man replied, *'I do believe; help me overcome my unbelief!'* (**Mark 9:24, NIV**).

Jesus healed the boy by telling the spirit to leave the body. He then held his hand and helped him up.

The child in this story is likely to have suffered from epilepsy, but back then, such illnesses were believed to have been caused by demon possessions. As a result, the ill were shunned by society, yet Jesus did not discriminate against them. Christianity teaches that faith makes anything possible.

The Widow at The Treasury (Mark 12:41-44)

Jesus was at the Temple watching people donate their money. A number of rich people donated vast amounts of money, but a vulnerable widow came along and gave *'two very small copper coins, worth only a few cents.'* (**Mark 12:42, NIV**).

Witnessing this, Jesus called his disciples to him and said, *'Truly I tell you, this poor widow has put more into the treasury than all the others. They all gave out of their wealth; but she, out of her poverty, put in everything—all she had to live on.'* (**Mark 12:43-44, NIV**)

The widow showed that she had full faith that God would provide for her even with no money left to live on. Christianity teaches that God will always provide for those who have faith.

The Anointing at Bethany (Mark 14:1-9)

Jesus was in Bethany at the home of Simon the Leper, when a woman arrived *'with an alabaster jar of very expensive perfume, made of pure nard.'* (**Mark 14:3, NIV**). She broke the bottle and poured the perfume (worth an entire average year's wages) over Jesus's head.

This made people angry – they said that she was wrong to waste the perfume as the money made from selling it could have been used to help the poor and needy. However, Jesus defended her.

'"Leave her alone,' said Jesus. 'Why are you bothering her? She has done a beautiful thing to me.'" (**Mark 14:6, NIV**).

Jesus pointed out that people can help the poor and needy any time as they will always be there; he, however, will not. Jesus saw the kindness in the woman's act and showed his appreciation.

Being at the home of Simon the Leper demonstrates Jesus's willingness to treat all members of society with equal love and respect, when others may have shunned Simon as unclean.

Faith & Discipleship

The word disciple means 'follower' or 'one who learns' and can refer to anyone who follows the teachings of Jesus. Throughout his life, Jesus had many disciples.

At the beginning of his ministry, Jesus chose twelve specific disciples to preach the Word of God. Unlike other Jewish teachers who might have chosen well-educated people, Jesus's first disciples were unschooled working men, some of whom had been disregarded by society. The jobs of these people or how they had acted in the past did not matter to Jesus.

The Call of the Disciples (Mark 1:16-20)

Simon (who later became Peter) and Andrew were fishermen and Jesus's first disciples. Seeing them as he walked to the Sea of Galilee, he called out, *'Come, follow me...and I will send you out to fish for people.'* **(Mark 1:17, NIV)**. Without hesitation, the men followed.

When he had gone a little farther, he saw two more fishermen, James and John. Without delay he called them, and they left their father, Zebedee, in the boat to follow Jesus.

The men all followed Jesus, giving up everything to become disciples. Christians believe they should follow the example of the disciples, wholeheartedly following Jesus and spreading the Word of God.

The Mission of the Twelve (Mark 6:7-13)

Jesus sent his disciples out in pairs to preach, heal people and get rid of demons. They were instructed to take nothing *'except a staff — no bread, no bag, no money...Wear sandals but not an extra shirt.'* **(Mark 6:8-9, NIV)**. They were to rely on their faith and the kindness of others to get by.

Jesus told them that if somebody made them feel unwelcome, they should leave. If these people chose to refuse the message of Jesus, the disciples didn't need to spend any more time with them.

Most of Jesus's mission with his disciples involved travelling, preaching and healing the sick. Today, it serves to inspire modern Christians who share their faith either personally or through missions with major organisations such as CAFOD and Christian Solidarity Worldwide.

The Cost and Rewards of Discipleship (Mark 8:34-38, 10:28-31)

Jesus was very clear that through following him, people would be rewarded both on Earth and with eternal life in heaven. Jesus also warned that the price of discipleship would be great. His disciples could expect to be persecuted and suffer in life, but this was a small price to pay for the reward.

'...no one who has left home...for me and the gospel will fail to receive a hundred times as much in this present age: homes, brothers, sisters, mothers, children and fields – along with persecutions – and in the age to come eternal life.' **(Mark 10:29-31, NIV)**

Those who chose a life of sin and temptation would not receive reward and favour on the Day of Judgement.

Jesus's followers risked being killed, and many were, particularly in the early days during the Roman Empire's rule. Today, Christians are still the most persecuted religious group in the world.

daydream
EDUCATION

The Woman with a Haemorrhage (Mark 5:24-34)

Amongst a large crowd who were following Jesus was a woman who was suffering from a haemorrhage. She hadn't stopped bleeding for twelve years and was growing worse.

Believing that Jesus had the power to heal her, she touched his cloak without telling him, and immediately she was healed.

Jesus felt his power leave him and asked the crowd who had touched him. The woman was afraid, fell to her knees and admitted that it was her. Jesus was not concerned by being touched by a woman who was seen by society as unclean. He simply said, *'Daughter, your faith has healed you. Go in peace and be freed from your suffering.'* **(Mark 5:34, NIV)**

This story represents the importance of faith and trusting in God's power.

Peter's Denials (Mark 14:27-31, 66-72)

At the last supper, Jesus predicted that his disciples would abandon him. Peter rebuked this claim, stating, *'Even if all fall away, I will not!'* **(Mark 14:29, NIV)**, but Jesus was adamant:

"'Truly I tell you,' Jesus answered, 'today – yes, tonight – before the rooster crows twice you yourself will disown me three times.'" **(Mark 14:30, NIV)**

The next day after Jesus was arrested, Peter denied knowing Jesus on three occasions. It wasn't until he heard the rooster crow twice that he realised what he had done. Horrified, Peter broke down.

Peter's denial carries an important message for Christians. The denial not only allowed him to survive so that he could continue the work of Jesus, but also demonstrated that even the most loyal of Christians will sometimes struggle with their faith.

The Commission and Ascension (Mark 16:14-20)

After his resurrection, Jesus appeared to his eleven disciples (Judas had left after betraying Jesus) to give them his final instructions. Jesus rebuked his followers for questioning their faith and not believing the people who had claimed to have seen him. He then gave them the Great Commission. Jesus promised that if the disciples carried out the Great Commission, great things would happen, but those who disbelieved would be condemned:

'Go into all the world and preach the gospel to all creation. Whoever believes and is baptized will be saved, but whoever does not believe will be condemned. And these signs will accompany those who believe: in my name they will cast out demons; they will speak in new tongues; they will pick up serpents with their hands; and if they drink any deadly poison, it will not hurt them; they will lay their hands on the sick, and they will recover.' **(Mark 16:15-18, NIV)**

He then **ascended** (went up) to heaven and sat down at the right hand of God.

To make *'disciples of all nations'* is a responsibility passed on to all Christians. The Church has an important role in evangelism, the spreading of the Christian faith.

daydream EDUCATION

Index

Index

Notes

Notes